Change Your Life!

The CORE Approach™ to Creating the Life You Want

How to Overcome the Obstacles and
Fears that Keep You from Your Dreams

Deborah Moses

Veris Associates, Inc.
Lansdale, Pennsylvania

Published by Insight Publishing Company
P.O. Box 4189
Sevierville, Tennessee 37864

Cover Design by Chavah Redmond, Sleeper Interactive

10 9 8 7 6 5 4 3 2

Printed in the United States of America

ISBN: 1-932863-13-3

To my heavenly Father:
With You, all things are possible.

To Mike,
my source of love, support, encouragement, and courage.

You have, however reluctantly at times, willingly undertaken a
myriad of roles throughout this process, including co-conspirator,
advisor, idea mirror, bartender, challenger, advocate, proofreader,
investor, and editor. You make me better than I could ever be
without you.

Thank you, Love.

TABLE OF CONTENTS

About the Author

Deborah Moses is the founder and President of Veris Associates, Inc. and Transforming U Seminars. Originally, she had no intention of writing a book, but simply intended to create training programs, bringing to others the experience she had gained, to help them avoid the inevitable pitfalls of learning the difficult way — by experience.

As more and more people asked how she created her businesses, it became evident that the system used by Deborah was not one that people came to instinctively, and she decided that a book was one of the best ways to reach a number of people. The intent became to reach as many as possible who desire to make changes, and need a process to follow. Thus, The CORE Approach™ was born.

A life and career as a student, consultant, business owner, researcher, teacher, trainer, partner, and parent have provided the credentials for her expertise, along with the schools she attended. Deborah attended Montgomery County Community College (Pennsylvania) and Temple University, and has furthered her education with certification programs in management, project management, leadership, and information technology.

In addition to running the businesses, speaking on a variety of topics at conferences and seminars, and writing, Deborah's current roles include those of wife to Mike, and mom to Michael, Jr., Kevin, Jason, and Christina, respectively. Those roles are the ones that come first and foremost in her life.

Foreword

As a published author and professional speaker, I get a wide variety of requests. They range from simple assistance to financing dreams. I feel compelled to consider all of the requests I receive, since my business is helping others succeed. I never know when one of these requests, and perhaps my role in making it a reality, might be just the one that makes the history books of the future.

Being asked to write a foreword for someone else's book is an interesting request. As authors, we have no difficulty writing our own ideas and thoughts. Writing a foreword is an honor and a responsibility. It is not a request to be taken lightly.

I meet many people in my travels and my seminars. A few stand out. The ones who stand out are the ones who have identified their dream, know that their dream will help others and that they have a message to convey. These are the people who have the courage, skill, passion, and perseverance to pursue it and make it a reality. The author of this book stands out.

There are many roads to success. Each person's travels are different. The CORE Approach™ provides a common-sense, four-step strategy that any person desiring change can follow. The concepts of Choice, Opportunity, Responsibility, and Expectation are basic concepts of life which, when combined in this fashion, make perfect sense as a recipe for success.

Deborah has been blessed with an ability to communicate the strategy she adopted. Her capacity for success is evident in the results of the projects she has undertaken. She's a forward thinker who has just begun to let the world know how effective she, and they, can be. Read the book. Adopt the concepts. They've been written for you by a respected, knowledgeable colleague who has done her homework and is now passing it on to you.

As with any new knowledge, it might take time to create all of these new habits in your life, but they are good, solid concepts that will help you achieve whatever it is you set out to achieve. There may be — probably will be — setbacks, but as Deborah writes, if you identify the obstacles, and the fears causing them, and work through them, you can move forward, taking the next step toward your goal choices. I've watched these concepts work for the author — they will also work for you.

Don't let that wicked witch scare you.

John Childers

John Childers is best known for his 4-day seminar, The "Million-Dollar Speaker" Training. (www.johnchilders.com) He is an author and creator of many live seminars and home study courses, and has helped launch the speaking careers of hundreds of professionals. A millionaire by age 37, John still teaches the real estate techniques he used to attain that goal, in addition to speaking on the same platforms in North America and Australia with other highly successful speakers including Mark Victor Hansen, Zig Ziglar, Robert Allen, Les Brown.

Disclaimer

The material contained in this book is a guide for those of you who want to make changes in your life. It is based on years and years of experiences, research, and my ultimate desire to help people. My hope is that it will help you in the ways you find most useful.

I want to be clear about one thing right up front. There are references to "leaps of faith," "prayer," "my God-given talents," and so forth. I have neither intention nor desire to offend anyone of any faith, religion, or belief system. My belief is in God, and so I talk about faith from that frame of reference.

Statistics indicate that most people have faith in a higher power than themselves. Whatever your belief, and whatever, or whomever, you refer to as your higher power, is just fine with me.

If you have no faith in any higher power, I pray that you will find one to believe in that is all that represents good to you. And I trust that you will use your faith to your advantage as you move through the exploration of identifying the changes you want to make in your life, and then pursuing those changes.

Acknowledgements

Having had so much help in recent months to get to the point of finishing and publishing this book, I would be remiss if I did not acknowledge those who helped me all or part of the way.

John Strelecky and Tom Antion, both of you have been so helpful and patient with my questions about how to do this or that.

Scott Schilling—my friend and colleague—thanks for continuing to be my "sounding board" partner, and letting me be yours.

Dan Poynter, I thank you for writing such a comprehensive book on publishing so that would-be authors in the novice state can see that there is a logical guide and not let the fear become paralyzing. And thanks for answering the phone in the wee hours of a California morning when Rita called you from the east coast!

Rita, for your patience and perseverance in understanding the steps to get this to the published state! And for keeping me organized.

Chavah and Tim: Thank you, thank you, thank you. You have no idea how incredibly important you have been to me throughout this process.

If I had to worry about everything with the business at the same time I was trying to complete this book, it would have gotten done, but I would no longer be sane. Although we don't always agree, Bill, you are always my sanity, sometimes my memory, and occasionally my brain, but first and foremost, my friend.

I have to acknowledge my friend and colleague, Cheryl, for the ability to always make me laugh. No matter what the day brings, I can always count on you to make me laugh out loud with one of your stories, your jokes, or sometimes just the crazy looks you get on your face. Thanks for always being there. You're a good friend.

Christina, for pitching in, even if you did roll your eyes sometimes, when I was busy trying to finish this and get it to the publisher. You are the best daughter a mom could ever have, and I love you.

To the rest of the Moses-Elton family, thanks for basically staying out of my hair (and out of trouble) so that I could get this accomplished!

John Childers—without you I'd still just be thinking about being an author and speaker, rather than living it. Thank you for your mentoring, belief, and support. You are a blessing to those of us who believe that God will help us and bless us if we work on the things we need to work on ourselves.

For Mom, and the rest of you out there who prayed...prayer works.

And Mike, you are my rock, and my forever love. Thanks for believing in me, helping by actually doing something or by leaving me alone, and for not letting me know how much you were worrying about how it would all work out. I wonder what would have happened if neither of us had learned to play golf...?

Author's note: When quotes are indicated, and the birth and death dates are not listed, the person quoted was alive at the time of this writing, but birth date was not readily available to the researchers.

"Go confidently in the direction of your dreams. Live the life you have imagined."
Henry David Thoreau (1817-1862)

Chapter 1   So, You Want to Change Your Life!

Chances are, your life isn't exactly what you thought it would be, or you wouldn't be reading this book. People want to make changes. It seems that we are seldom satisfied with our lot in life. Why is that?

My belief is that this is because we end up in roles and jobs and careers to which we aren't suited for a variety of reasons. We find that those roles, jobs, and careers aren't satisfying to us because they don't have close enough ties to our true paths in life—the paths that are determined by paying attention to what ignites our passions.

We end up in these unsatisfying places through a multitude of journeys. Many of us start on the wrong path in our college years because someone convinces us that some career path is more lucrative than another in which we have more interest. Or, we follow the advice of a parent we respect or don't want to disappoint. Sometimes we even convince ourselves that the path we are on is the right one, because we've gotten good at pushing those things that really excite us beneath the surface.

Some of us go through school pursuing our dreams, or what we think they are, only to discover that the reality of the dream is not the same as the fictionalized version. This would be the version we had in our minds before we knew what the day-to-day reality would be. When this happens, individuals generally spend time, usually years, in this career before determining that it's not the right one for them.

Others start with a job at an early age, either after their schooling ends, or while they are in school, and continue with that job or that company for some period of time, often their entire working life.

I've heard people say that they can't wait to retire because they hate the job they have to go to every day. How sad it is that there are individuals who don't realize that they could make another choice for themselves, or that they could have made a different one earlier in their lives.

We find ourselves, often between the ages of 35 and 55, in a life situation, career, or location in which we are not happy, fulfilled, or nurtured.

The same can be said of relationships, home locations and type of housing, personal characteristics and behaviors, expectations, financial situations, or anything else that you can think of that people want to change.

We get into a specific "zone" which is familiar. Some would call this our comfort zone. However, even when *familiar* doesn't equate with *comfortable*, we stay. Why? If where we are is not comfortable, why do we stay there? The answer is that in general, it is easier to remain in the familiar.

Whatever routes we take to arrive at that familiar zone, many of us eventually get there, and realize after some period of time that we aren't where we want to be or where we thought we would be. Which is probably where you are about now — right?

Maybe it's not you who wants the change. Perhaps you know someone, or you are married to someone who is not satisfied with his or her life, and you're trying to understand and help. Hang in there, and I'll see what I can do to clear all this up for you.

Change. Even though we tend to stay in the familiar, it seems our lives are constantly full of change. We get married and have to adjust to living with someone else. We get divorced and have to adjust to living alone. We have children, and experience all the changes (life changes as well as diaper changes!) that go along with raising them. Our employers expand and downsize. Our roles change as these events take place. We take on roles as community leader, coach, fund-raiser, or committee member. Life is full of change, yet here we are talking about changing even more.

So, why are you reading this book? What is it that you wish to change? Perhaps you don't even know yet. You just feel as though your life is not complete, fulfilled, or satisfied. As you read on, perhaps it will become clear to you.

Some common catalysts for change are:

- I'm single and I want to be married and settle down.
- I don't like my job.
- My career isn't what I thought it would be.
- I want to be a better parent to my children.
- I'm not making enough money.
- I'm married and think I'd be happier divorced.
- I have talent I don't use and don't know how to make a living with, but I want to use it.
- I'm overweight and I'm worried about my health.
- I want to do something that I love.
- I know I'm not being the best person I can be.
- I need a better balance between my work and home life.

There are others, but my guess is that one of these has a ring of truth for you.

The first step in all of this is identifying what it is that feels "wrong" and explore your thoughts about what changes you need to make in order for it to be "right."

There are many ways to do this, and we'll explore a few of them. As you go through these pages, keep a notebook or journal nearby. You'll be asked to think about things and make some lists, and you may want to make notes to help you navigate through the process of change.

The first thing you are going to write in your notebook is a list. Make a list of the things in your life with which you are unsatisfied. What changes do you want to make in regard to the items on your list? This is usually not a list you can make in five minutes. Take your time, and refer back to it as you think of things to add later.

There are just a few items left on my list of things with which I am unsatisfied. One of them concerns how much exercise I need versus how much exercise I regularly manage to fit into my schedule. I need to make a change in order to be satisfied. The change listed is "Make time to exercise at least two hours each week."

Change is good. You will see this statement in this book numerous times. Tell yourself, *change is good*. Tell others. Eventually you'll convince yourself.

Think about it. If everything stayed the same, if we didn't learn and grow and change, our very existence would be rather boring, wouldn't it? Now, there are those who will tell you that boring is not so bad—that the comfort zone of the familiar is what they want.

I don't buy it for a second. There are times in our lives when there has been too much change, and for a period we need the situations and people in our lives to be stable. That works for some period of time. But stable is not the same as boring.

Boring implies that everything stays the same, day in and day out, for weeks, months, or perhaps years. Just because it's a familiar zone doesn't mean it's good for us or even that it's a positive influence in our lives.

What is the impetus for change? For some, it is a realization, as we said above, that life is not what was expected; these people generally want a change that will allow them to feel different than they feel now. There is usually a satisfaction component to their search.

For others, an event has triggered the change process. Many times this comes in the form of a loss experienced by the individual. The loss can be personal, as in a death of a loved one, or professional, as in the loss of a job. Losses involve circumstance or situation changes, and they force the individual to think about how the future will be different.

It all boils down to the fact that we either jump or we are pushed. Either way, change has to be faced, evaluated, and acted upon.

Think about why you chose this book. What changes are you facing? Why does changing your life seem attractive to you? Regardless of whether you are jumping into this change, or being pushed into it, The CORE Approach™ is a process that you can follow. Following the four step process will allow you to navigate more easily, with more insight, and fewer setbacks, than muddling through without a process to follow.

Dealing with change involves transitions and transformations that include your thoughts, feelings, words, and actions. There are few individuals who are comfortable evaluating all of these things. The Myers-Briggs Personality Inventory, and other personality assessments identify our specific strengths and preferences in dealing with ourselves and others.

For example, you will approach change differently if you are a "thinking" person than if you are a "feeling" person. There are few people who really enjoy change. Change, by its very nature, implies a lack of familiarity. Unfamiliar situations and circumstances can increase stress levels. Thus, we conclude that change is stressful.

Change does not have to be stressful. It *seems* stressful when it is approached in an unstructured manner. Having a four-step process increases the likelihood that the change will be enjoyable rather than stressful.

"Not everything that is faced can be changed, but nothing can be changed until it is faced."
James A. Baldwin (1924-1987)

Chapter 2   The Scary Nature of Change

According to Webster, in *Webster's New Twentieth Century Dictionary*, the first four meanings for the word *change* are:

1. Any variation or alteration in form, state, quality or essence; or, a passing from one state to another.
2. Variety.
3. A succession of one thing in place of another.
4. The passing of one phase to another.

There are other meanings listed, but they all deal with the same basic concepts.

The *Oxford Dictionary* lists, as definitions for change:

1. The act, or an instance, of making or becoming different.
2. An alteration or modification.
3. A new experience; variety.

There are a few other definitions that either speak about a different type of meaning of the word (such as monetary change from a large denomination paper bill) or are variations on the same concept as those listed above.

Whether the discussion is about a variation of something that currently exists, moving to another phase, or making a complete substitution of one thing for another, we are dealing with change.

Change is a part of our lives. Our bodies change as we move through the stages of our lives. Our personalities change, along with our preferences for music, food, leisure time activities, and more as we go through life. Our lifestyles change as we become single adults or a couple, as we have children and grandchildren, or when we make a choice to live a single or alternate lifestyle. Even though as human beings we resist change, the reality is that our lives change all the time. We frequently don't recognize these shifts as change because they happen gradually, or they just "happen" to us. They are not always a result of our conscious choices.

Unconscious changes are the result of growth. When we decide that we like a new food for the first time, dress differently because of a new role in life, or even change our signature as we get older and view ourselves as "more sophisticated," these are not always conscious changes. These changes are commonly just integrated into the person we've become, and they become a new habit.

If you are reading this book, it is most likely because you are considering making deliberate, conscious changes in your life. This could be a pattern for you, or it might be the first time you've decided to make a big change. Either way, you may—like many people—feel resistant to change. We get into our comfortable places where life is status quo and the proverbial apple cart is not being upset, and we like that place. We like the familiar. We like being comfortable.

However, you may have decided that this familiar, comfortable place isn't satisfying for you, and change is desired. So, here you are—reading this book.

What do you need to know before we launch into the four- step CORE Approach™?

First and foremost, you can start wherever you are. Wherever you find yourself today, here and now, is the right place to start. You might think that you can't start something or you aren't sure what it is you want to change. Please understand that even if you don't yet know what changes you want or need to make, that's okay. That place of uncertainty is a starting place, a jumping off point.

You also need to know that this is not an absolute process; it is to be used as a guideline. Every situation will require a somewhat different application of the process, even though the basic concepts remain the same. This means that every person is different, and every situation of change is different. Who we are at various stages of our lives will determine which parts of the process — or which concepts — require greater attention, and which parts come to us more easily.

The first change using this new process will be the most difficult. Any new process takes time to understand, and once understood, takes time to learn to use. There will be setbacks as you fall into old habits and have to remind yourself that you have new habits to follow that are more effective than the old ones. There may be rude awakenings at times throughout the process of learning to work through change.

You need to know that you are not alone.

I can't tell you how many people have spoken to me over the years about the dissatisfaction they feel with their life in some way or another. If you feel this way, you are part of a large group of people who feel the need to have a more satisfied, balanced, or fulfilled life.

And you need to know that almost everyone believes that change is scary.

Why Change Causes Fear

Change is good.

If change is good, why does the thought of change cause fear? For exactly the reasons mentioned. We get comfortable. We dislike the unknown. We like being in the familiar. We dislike not knowing the outcome, or at least the potential outcome, of a situation. We prefer to deal with people we know well, so we can predict with some certainty how they will act and react. We like knowing what's coming our way, and having "normal" days that don't stress us. However, much of the time our normal, comfortable, typical, and predictable days are pretty darn stressful. That's a sure sign that change is needed!

> *"Change has a considerable psychological impact on the human mind. To the fearful it is threatening because it means that things may get worse. To the hopeful it is encouraging because things may get better. To the confident it is inspiring because the challenge exists to make things better."*
>
> **King Whitney, Jr.**
> **President, Personnel Laboratory Inc.**

Human beings resist change. It's a fact of life. Even when the typical day is consistently stressful, we resist making the necessary changes unless and until the changes are our idea, or so deeply desired that the stress of change isn't nearly as bad as the stress of things remaining the same. Still with me?

In other words, it frequently has to be potentially life-threatening stress in order to induce some people to make changes in their lives. These people know their lives need to change; they also know how resistant to change they can be. For them, the familiar "bad" life is better than the stress of making the changes that would enable them to have a more fulfilling life.

Most of us wouldn't categorize ourselves as "fearful" on a regular basis. But let's think about what *fear* is. Fear is a feeling of anxiety or agitation caused by the presence or nearness of danger, real or perceived. Maybe you don't think you feel fear. How often do you feel anxious or agitated? Irritated? Stressed? Not sure what to do about something? My guess is that you feel one or more of these emotions more often than you might be comfortable admitting.

How do you know that you are anxious? Do you have physical habits that arise when you are anxious? These manifest themselves in the form of eating, smoking, gum chewing, hair twisting, nail biting, finger drumming, pencil tapping, and other similar "nervous" behaviors.

Where does anxiety show itself in your body? We all have physical symptoms of anxiety, but we don't always realize it. People show symptoms of anxiety in different ways.

Does your anxiety present itself in your gut, in the form of stomach pains? Does it present itself as headaches, or migraines? Does your voice get high pitched or do you speak more quickly? Do your shoulders hurt, because your muscles are tight or because you hunch them up? Does your jaw ache from clenching your teeth? Pay attention to your particular physical sensations that accompany anxiety.

When I'm stressed, I feel it in the solar plexus area, which is between the ribs at the lower portion of the ribcage, in the center of the upper abdomen. It's a "butterflies" type of feeling, and when I feel it, I know that I have doubts or some type of anxiety about what I'm considering doing or saying. I also store tension in my shoulders, so I frequently have muscle spasms in the trapezius muscles across the top of the shoulder from the base of my neck. Any chiropractor or massage therapist who has worked with me will verify that!

Anxiety can present itself in many forms, and you need to pay attention to your body and your behaviors to determine the physical symptoms you manifest when anxious. Once you've determined how your anxiety presents itself, this will be another self-check about your decisions. If you are feeling anxious, the choice is probably hasty, ill-planned, or maybe just a bad idea. If you have no true feelings of anxiety, then the choice is probably a good one, or so new that you don't have sufficient information on which to base a sound opinion.

If you are a spiritual person, you can also check that "still, small voice" of your intuition, or God-voice, if you will. If there are no warning signs, either from the physical signs of anxiety, or if you are getting a green light (people get their intuitive senses in different ways), then you can trust that your choice is solid, and feel comfortable taking it to the next step.

Sometimes all that is required in order to go from being anxiety-laden to comfortable about a choice is time. We all want everything NOW. Timing is everything. How many times have you made a quick retort to something someone has said, and immediately wished you could take it back? Or you act on a decision, and then realize later that you should have thought it through a bit more. If you have any doubt about your choice, then wait. Chances are that is what you are supposed to do.

My belief is that the universe, God, or whatever you believe to be your higher authority will let you know when the time is right to act on your choices. You have to pay attention and listen. These messages are easy to miss, especially if we are not conditioned to be seeking them. When we insist upon acting before we have thought through a choice, or when we are feeling unsure about the rightness of moving forward, it is better to wait. Watch for the signs that the choice is solid by paying attention to your thoughts, your body, and what the world around you is communicating. Otherwise, you may be paralyzed by anxiety and fear. Or worse, you may move forward and quickly come to regret that decision.

The Paralysis of Fear

Before getting around to actually sitting down and writing this book, I got a whole lot of things accomplished. Let's see; all the Christmas shopping got done, as well as the seasonal decorating of the house, I wrote three of my monthly newsletters, repainted and redecorated my kitchen, cleaned my office, installed software on my computer, readied my accounting information for tax preparation, and completed a host of other not-as-important-as-my-book things. I was procrastinating in a big way, which I did not understand, because the three newsletters all dealt with The CORE Approach™ as the feature article.

What was holding me back from writing?

As a project manager, and then a manager of project managers, I have learned one thing about myself: getting started often feels overwhelming, even when I *want* to get started. That's what was going on with this book. Even though I thought about it constantly, wrote pieces of it in my head during car rides and while stretching out in bed at night, dreamt about it, and even wrote snippets on napkins in restaurants, I couldn't seem to get my head around getting started.

Twice I sat down and started it, and twice I got as far as opening and saving a Word document entitled "The CORE Approach" before I became quite happily distracted by my e-mail or a phone call. It was very easy to allow myself to become separated from the task at hand. In fact, I took down all of the holiday decorations the morning of the day I actually started the writing in earnest. And that was after I had written for two hours!

So, one thing that can cause paralysis is a sense of being overwhelmed by what it will take to get started once you've made a choice to change. If you research the word overwhelmed you find that awe-inspiring is one of the synonyms. If you look up awe there are two types of words listed, one being fear-related and one being wonder-related. So, in actuality, although being overwhelmed doesn't really feel like fear, it's closely related.

The actual fear, for me, I believe, has to do with whether or not I will be able to accomplish the project I set out to do. Not just writing, but any project. It also includes a sense of not knowing exactly what will happen during the project, which breaks down to a fear of the unknown. This, from me! I'm someone who, for all intents and purposes, is seen as a risk-taker and rather daring individual.

The point is that fear comes in all shapes and sizes and for all types of reasons. The reasons can be based on the reality of past experience, or some sort of perceived danger. They can stem from having heard a comment someone made many, many years ago about something you did, or from an actual failure you experienced in a similar circumstance. The range of origins of our fears is boundless.

> *"Fear is a question: What are you afraid of, and why?*
> *Just as the seed of health is in illness, because illness*
> *contains information, your fears are a treasure house of*
> *self-knowledge if you explore them."*
>
> **Marilyn Ferguson (1938-)**
> **Editor and Publisher of "Brain/Mind Bulletin"**

Exploring fear requires an understanding of the types of fears that can be present. There are real fears and there are perceived fears.

Typical real fears about change usually include past failure, evidenced by experiencing physical, financial, or emotional harm; or having experienced punishment, rebuke, or teasing; failure that resulted in harm in some way to another person; a change that resulted in a negative experience; lack of knowledge about the choice we've made.

Perceived fears about change usually include the unknown result, and therefore potential for failure; others' reactions; not knowing if the circumstances from the past remain the same; potential for success.

Any statement or question that can be started with the words, "What if..." will generally have a fear associated with it. This is fear of the unknown at its worst.

What would seem to be a small, insignificant passing comment to one person may be a single instance of personal insult or emotional pain that paralyzes another for years. Only you can determine whether the obstacle you are experiencing is from fear that has grown from past emotional experiences, actual trials that failed, the unrealistic fear of the unknown, or some other cause. It is worth the time to investigate, including using introspective techniques, to determine where the fear comes from. Only after identifying the fear and its cause—if there is a real cause—can you begin to deal with eliminating the fear.

A real fear is fear that exists when an actual danger is present. You feel fear when you drive your car across an intersection and a car is going through a stop sign and heading directly toward your car. You feel actual fear when you are in the middle of acting on a life decision and you find out information that will cause failure. Real fear is felt if your child is sick or in an accident.

Perceived fear is often referred to as neurotic fear. This is the "what-if" type of fear. What if I marry her and find out that she's not perfect? What if my children can't read when they get to first grade? What if I take on that project and then it doesn't turn out the way I think (or "they" think) it should? What if I change careers and don't like the new career? Or even worse, what if I make changes and find out that I'm not good at the new changes?

One of the fears that stops us dead in our tracks and keeps us from asking intelligent questions or speaking up with a comment or opinion, whether it is in school, a meeting at our office, or in our own family, is: "What if I'm wrong?" We are so afraid of sounding silly or uneducated, and in fact, of being wrong, that we often fail to get or give needed information.

"To live a creative life, we must lose our fear of being wrong."

Joseph Chilton Pearce
Bestselling author and speaker on human
intelligence, creativity, and learning

Perceived fear also creeps up when we are faced with a choice about a situation similar to one that turned out badly in the past. In this case, an evaluation needs to be made in relation to whether or not the circumstances of the current situation are the same as, or different from, the previous situation.

In other words, if the fear is from a past experience, then the responsive action is to determine whether the root cause of that negative past experience still exists. The alternative could be that time and circumstances have made that past experience an unrealistic possibility in the present case.

It's really about evaluating the risk involved. If your assessment of the risk reveals that the circumstances are significantly different from the situation that occurred in the past, then it requires review to determine whether the level of risk is now acceptable.

If the fear is from perception, then the responsive action is to determine the root of the perceived danger. Ask yourself, "Why do I have this fear?" The "what-ifs" can keep you paralyzed for a very long time if you let them.

In overcoming the paralysis that kept me from beginning projects, or from starting this book, I learned to become fairly accurate at the risk assessment that allowed me to determine whether or not the risk was acceptable to move forward. When I chose to move forward, I began over time to use the Nike tag line "Just Do It." Once I sat down and started laying out the project, it always fell into place. It was getting started that got to me.

Many times the task at hand seems daunting. We think things like:
- It's going to take a lot of time.
- It's going to take a lot of energy.
- It's going to be harder than I even know at this point.

What we are really thinking is that we're afraid of how much of our time it will take, or how much of our energy it will consume, or how difficult it will be. We're afraid that maybe we aren't up to the task; perhaps we don't want to admit that we're lazy. What we're really afraid of is what we will have to relinquish in order to accomplish the change goal that we've chosen.

These fears stem back to the fear of giving up the familiar and the comfortable, even though the comfortable may not be especially good for us.

Insight about your previous accomplishments and failures will provide the information needed to get through present fears. How have you dealt with things in the past? Do you have a history of not completing things you start? Do people know you as someone who jumps into things before having thought them through, thus getting into trouble mid-stream? Or have you always performed above expectations, and now perhaps you fear that you can't live up to past accomplishments?

What is holding you back?

As you can see, there could be as many reasons for fear paralysis as there are people who are paralyzed by fear. The causes are numerous, often unique, and frequently reoccurring to an individual. The good news is that paralysis is able to be overcome with introspection, insight and determination.

Many people who are paralyzed by fear are the people we commonly refer to as "control freaks." These people are so immersed in controlling each and every aspect of their environment and their life that simply thinking about changes in their lives can send them into a tailspin. Controlling people have a lot of difficulty with change, because it is the unknown result of the change that causes fear.

One seemingly paradoxical fear is the fear of success. If you try something and succeed, things will change. If things change, your relationships will change, and you may be unable to predict what those changes will be or how they will affect you or those close to you.

If you become successful at your chosen change, what will you do next to follow it up?

These, and other fears, can be stifling when we are in the midst of them. By using a system to decipher them, taking a step back, and perhaps enlisting the aid of someone less emotionally involved in the situation, we can make them less scary and more manageable.

Overcoming Fear as a Precursor to Change

When talking about change, it is not always apparent that those things which hold us back are based in fear. We see obstacles in our path, and we can identify and verbalize those obstacles to others. Only when we spend time exploring the origin of the obstacle do we understand that obstacles are generally self-imposed and fear based.

Thom Rutledge, in his book *Embracing FEAR and Finding the Courage to Live Your Life*, talks about steps to overcoming fear, using the acronym F.E.A.R. The concepts he outlines are Facing, Exploring, Accepting, and Responding to the fear in order to have courage. You cannot face fear if you don't acknowledge that it exists, which is why you need to break down what you are thinking and feeling into manageable actions to which you can then respond. Once you know what you are dealing with, and that what you are feeling is actually fear, then you can explore it, as discussed in the sections above.

Exploring the root cause, determining whether the fear is real or perceived (neurotic), and then working through the basis for the fear is the exploring phase. Accepting that we all have fears and accepting our own fears goes a long way toward being able to work through the fear or overcome it. We can then respond in an appropriate manner, by accepting that the fear is there and moving through it anyway; or we can respond by breaking it down until it is no longer a fear, which therefore no longer holds us hostage. Once the fear is gone, the response is easier and there are more options.

Some people cannot admit that they have what they perceive to be shortcomings. Fear is often considered a shortcoming, or weakness, and therefore many of us have a very difficult time admitting to feeling fear of any type. Let me assure you: There's not a human being alive who has not felt, or does not feel, fear.

We all have fears. Some people just learn to deal with them or cover them up better than others. And some people get over them by going through a specific process, as outlined by Mr. Rutledge or some other authority, either individually or through therapeutic intervention. For those of you whose fears are so severe or overwhelming that you are prevented from living your life, I urge you to seek professional help. There are extreme fears, identified as phobias, which absolutely require professional help. This book is not designed to deal with "clinical" fears. If you feel you have an extreme fear that is clinical in nature, please speak with your health care professionals to determine the best course of action.

The types of fears dealt with by using The CORE Approach™ are the more benign fears that exist within all of us at different times. These are the fears that we might not be smart enough, good enough, or "something" enough to be successful. These are the fears that we'll lose favor in the eyes of someone we care about because of some action or lack of action on our part. These fears are present in varying degrees for all of us, depending upon our background and experiences.

Our discomfort with the unfamiliar is fear. When we discuss fear in relation to change, we see that fears manifest themselves in the obstacles that we create or that we perceive to be blocking our ability to make changes.

Once there is insight that fear exists and has to be faced, it can be explored. Once explored, it can then be dealt with and accepted or alleviated. Acceptance is the key to moving forward and eliminating the paralysis of the fear. Learning how to respond to the fear, once or on an ongoing basis, is the key to moving forward. Thank you, Mr. Rutledge, for your straightforward breakdown of the FEAR acronym.

At this point, you might be thinking that I'm a little bit crazy. Fear as the basis of our stumbling blocks and obstacles? You might say something like this:

> **But I'm not *afraid* of anything, I just can't quit my job (and start my own business, or change careers, or go back to school, or significantly alter a lifestyle in order to lose weight) right now. It's not practical. My family needs me.**

Hear me out. Read on. Many people replace fear with rationalization in order to not appear weak—even in their own eyes. We're taught to be strong and not to be afraid of anything. Do the following taunts sound familiar?

"Big boys don't cry."
"Come on, don't be a chicken!"
"Are you crazy? You can't do that!"
"You won't do it—you're a scaredy-cat!"

"You don't really think you could do that, do you?"

We learn our fears based on this type of comment. In addition, there are the comments after the fact, when what we accomplished was seen as "not good enough" in some fashion:

"I told you that wouldn't work."
"Why don't you listen to me? You can't do _____ well at all!"
"What on earth made you think you could do that?"

Is any of this ringing a bell in your mind? I hope not, but unfortunately, most of us have heard these messages from someone at some time. These messages from the past often have the result of causing fears in the future.

Fear is a natural human emotion. The types of fears we have been discussing are normal and expected. There are those fears that are excessive and require therapeutic intervention, as mentioned earlier. The CORE Approach™ deals with the typical fear that a relatively well-adjusted person feels when faced with change.

We don't always recognize it as fear. But everyone feels it to some degree. The difference is that not everyone admits it.

Here are some steps to help you when you feel "stuck":

- Take the time to determine how you can begin to recognize fear when it presents itself in your life. Let it be. Know that it is there.
- Take the time to determine whether it is a rational or an irrational fear.
- If it is rational, identify where the fear originated.
- Think about whether the original circumstances are currently present, or whether there are different circumstances now.

- Identify the risk you would take by taking action in spite of the fear. Listen to your body and to the affirmations or warnings you hear and see around you.
- Make a conscious choice to wait, and continue to assess whether the risk is real, or whether you should move forward and act on your choice.

"Do what you feel in your heart to be right—for you'll be criticized anyway. You'll be damned if you do, and damned if you don't."

Eleanor Roosevelt (1884-1962)

Chapter 3   Get Real with Yourself

What do you think of when you think of obstacles? Perhaps you picture an obstacle course as something to go through as part of a physical education class in school, perhaps a military boot camp obstacle course, or maybe you've been on teambuilding events or scouting events where you had an obstacle course to run. The obstacle course elements in your way are difficult to navigate through or around, and are purposely put there to discourage you or to provide specific challenges.

An obstacle is something that blocks the way. Obstacles hold us back. So, when we think about obstacles in our lives—what types of barriers are there? And who put them there?

Let me get right to the point here: One type of obstacle in your life is all the "baggage" you've picked up in your years on this earth. As a young adult, based on the law of averages, you probably have less baggage than if you are an older adult. Generally speaking, the older we get, the more baggage we tend to accumulate.

Definition of baggage: All the negative messages other people would have us believe about ourselves.

One thing I've learned through the years is that we are *very* good at believing bad stuff about ourselves. Conversely, we are not good at believing good things about ourselves, even when we know intellectually that these good things are true. Hence, the power of baggage.

And by the way, guess who put all that baggage there? I'll bet that you are going to say that all the people who gave you the negative messages put the baggage there...right? Wrong! YOU put that baggage there. And the reason you put it there is because you believed the negative messages. Stop sabotaging yourself by believing negative messages about yourself.

Positive Statements Versus Baggage

In seminars, this is the time when I ask the participants to write their "Things at which I excel" list. This is a list of at least 30 things that are good about the participant or at which they excel. So, pull out your notebook and start listing. Write the numbers 1 through 30 down the left side of the page, and list your talents, positive characteristics, appearance, anything about yourself that you believe is good.

If you can write more than 30, keep going and write as many as you possibly can. Take sufficient time to do this exercise. It is an important step in learning how to make positive changes in your life and create the life you want. If you have trouble getting your list up to 30 items, here are some suggestions:

1. Think about all the roles in your life. Perhaps you are a mother, sister, daughter, father, son, brother, grandparent, manager, banker, cook, errand runner, driver, cleaning person, teacher, lay religious leader, speaker, committee chairperson, researcher, decorator, gardener, landscaper, painter, etc. Think about home, work, family, hobbies, likes and dislikes, favorite ways to relax, and all the other things that don't come to mind easily. This will begin to open up your thought processes.

2. Think about what roles you'd rather have than the ones you have now, or think about the roles you'd like to have

in addition to the ones you have now. These could be roles at volunteer events you might be thinking about participating in, clubs or organizations you would like to join, or other things you have not yet achieved in your life that you would like to achieve. This will give you more information about what you think you are good at, since we all tend to gravitate toward roles at which we think we can succeed.

3. Think about your dreams. If you were doing what you love, what would that be? Is this something at which you excel? It probably is.

4. Ask others what they think. Start with your family members or co-workers and ask, "With all that you know about me, what do you think I do well?" Don't judge their answers or argue with them about whether their observations are accurate or not in your opinion. Be graceful, say "thank you" for the compliment, write down what they said on your list, and move on to the next good thing about you.

At this point, you should have at least 30 things on your list that you know you do well. Hopefully, if you've done all of the things suggested, you have more than one page completed!

How many good things are on your list?

How easy or difficult was this exercise for you?

For most people this is not an easy exercise. We are socialized from a very early age not to brag, not to say good things about ourselves because it will sound like boasting, so we have difficulty making these observations about ourselves. We have even more difficulty believing them, even when we can list them.

If you haven't come up with 30, don't keep reading. Stop, go back to your list, and come up with at least 30 before you read on.

Now that you have a list of many things at which you excel, think about how many of the items on that list you truly believe. Be honest. Do you believe they are all true? If you answered no, why don't you believe these things? Think about this. What will help you believe the things others see in you? Sometimes all it takes is a realization that it is fine to admit that there are things at which you excel. Give yourself permission to believe these good things. Take the permission I am officially giving you to actually know these things about yourself. Successful people are those who are confident about their abilities.

Perhaps it takes a little more effort to truly believe in your entire list. If so, spend some time repeating the list in a positive, affirming manner. This would sound something like, "I am a good listener. I am good at playing basketball. I am a good friend. I am a wonderful gardener." And so on. If it helps, say these things while viewing yourself in a mirror. You may feel a little silly, but many people find that this method helps them to believe these positive things about themselves.

You may have to do this several times, before any of it feels natural. It takes some people longer than others to believe in themselves. How long it takes to begin believing in yourself depends entirely on how confident you are to begin with, and how many achievements you accomplish along the way, once you begin this process of creating the life you want.

Now that you *know* at least a few things about yourself that are positive, even if it isn't the entire 30, let's move on. You have begun to conquer the first obstacle that we all face—baggage. You've started to conquer it by believing in yourself.

There are those of us who were raised to believe we could tackle anything that came our way, or we got that confidence by necessity. There are those of us who were raised to believe that nothing we could possibly do was right. And then there are those of us who fall somewhere between those two extremes.

Pick one or two of the things you wrote down that are good about you. Refer back to the list of changes you want to make about the lack of satisfaction in your life. The items you choose should be pertinent to the changes you want to make. Write these items in large letters on a clean piece of paper, as an affirmation—one affirmation to one sheet of paper, such as "I am an exceptional pianist." Now, put each one up where you will see it regularly. This may mean taping each one to a mirror, a wall in your office, your dashboard, or some other place prominent in your sight.

Each time you see one of these affirmations, stop for a second or two and repeat it to yourself. Whenever one comes to mind, even if it is not immediately in front of you, repeat it to yourself. As you do this, envision yourself doing whatever it is that you are doing excellently, and which you are affirming. Repeating affirmations to ourselves and envisioning them assists us in retaining the positive image in our minds.

There is significant power in the suggestions we provide to ourselves. These suggestions need to override all of the negative statements we've believed about ourselves for so many years.

For every negative thought you have about yourself from now on, replace it with a positive thought immediately. Mark Victor Hansen, co-author of the famous *Chicken Soup for the Soul* books, recommends waving your hand in the air, as if you are crossing out the negative, and saying "Cancel, cancel." Then say your positive affirmation.

Think about a method that would work for you. Would wearing a rubber band on your wrist remind you to repeat positive affirmations about yourself? What about having an accountability partner—someone with whom you spend a lot of time? This person could remind you when you identify a negative thought, and encourage you to repeat a positive thought or statement that cancels it out.

Or you could add positive thinking to your to-do list every day, so that you see it listed and remember to think positively. List it in your goals for the week. Do whatever works for you—make it your choice!

Regardless of the method you choose, begin to think positively about yourself, and remember that no one can make you think negatively about yourself. By acknowledging that the negative could even possibly be correct, you allow that to enter your psyche—your being, your soul—and it begins to become real. Thoughts and ideas can manifest reality if you let them. So, what we want to do is ensure that what we are manifesting is positive, which will come from positive thoughts and ideas.

If you immediately consider a way to turn a negative thought or statement into a positive statement, you can consider whether it has merit (as some constructive advice does) in a positive light, rather than under the clouds of negativity.

For instance, what if, while writing this book, a proof-editing friend or family member read a part of it and said, "I don't understand this section on negative thinking. It's a weird concept!" I would have a choice to be upset and feel criticized, or I could realize that it was not yet complete, and determine what else needed to go into that section in order to make it easier to understand and not seem weird. The second choice is the healthier and more positive of the two, don't you think?

Begin to think of criticism, or constructive suggestions, whether they come from within or from someone else, as opportunities to learn. Rather than think the negative, as I could have in the previous example if I considered, "I must not be able to write because they didn't understand that part," I could realize that the comment is a way to learn what it is that others need in order to understand. This will help perfect my writing style in a way that will benefit the reader, and also me, since it will make me a better writer. If the readers understand, and are consequently helped by the material in the book, chances are they will recommend the book to others.

Not only will I sell more books, but I will also have achieved my goal of helping someone, and potentially a lot more than one person!

Find a way to turn every negative thought into a positive one. It's amazing how powerful optimism can be.

> *"Perpetual optimism is a force multiplier."*
> **Colin Powell (1937-)**

Go back to your "Things at which I excel" list. Think about whether you answered yes or no when asked whether you believe all of the answers on the list. If you answered no to the question of whether you believe it all, think about that again. If you still don't believe you excel at all of the items on the list, think about why you don't believe. Then turn that statement into a positive statement by finding something positive to say about it, or by determining what you can learn from it.

For example, perhaps one of the things on your list is "I am a good father" but you don't believe you are always a good father.

Rather than continue to berate yourself for the areas in which you believe you fall short, seek an opportunity to relate to it positively. The thought process might go something like this:

"My wife says I'm a good father, but I don't believe it's true. I work too many hours and don't spend enough time with the kids. She does all the hard parenting."

"Okay, so I'm supposed to turn this into a positive statement, or learn from it. So...I'm a good father because I make time to coach the kids' teams for baseball and soccer. To eliminate the negative, I can learn to make being home earlier on weekday evenings a priority, so that I can spend more one-on-one time with each of the children. If I do this, I will feel better about my parenting, because I'm doing more than just working with them at the sports fields. "

"If I do this, an added benefit will be that I'll be a more supportive husband, because I'll be alleviating some of the parenting burden and my wife can take some time to do something for herself."

We all need to stop beating ourselves up over the things we know we should change, find a positive aspect in the negative statement, then act on the positive. When we learn to make this a habit, we soon find that there are fewer negatives, and as a result, we are happier and more at peace with our lives.

Try it a few times. It doesn't take long before it will become a habit, and you will be surprised by how good you feel.

> *"People who cannot make progress, despite knowing what they want to do, are sometimes paralyzed from fear. ...Being brave does not come from lack of fear, it comes from taking action despite fear."*
> **Diana Robinson, PhD, CCG**
> **Success Strategies Coach**

Facing Down the Obstacles One by One

There are a multitude of obstacle types, as you will see as you go through this book. Perhaps you will identify with some of them in thinking about your own life. I've tried to include the most common types on these pages. It would take another entire book to list them all. Maybe that will somehow turn into a sequel CORE Approach™ book!

Here are some common "obstacle" statements:

- I couldn't do that—I don't have the_____ (experience, training, talent, etc.).
- I can't afford to leave my current job to make the changes I want to make.
- My (spouse, parents, children, etc.) won't understand.
- What if I try it and find out it's not what I want?
- People will think I'm crazy!
- If I did that, it would turn my family upside down.
- I'll be criticized for taking chances!
- What I want to do isn't what my degree is in—how will I have any credibility?
- What if it doesn't work out?

- I'll only be happy if I follow my dream of _____(art, social work, whatever your passion might be).
- I'll never have enough money to have a vacation home.

What are the types of obstacles you may be facing? Although there may be significant obstacles in your life which you believe hold you back, in reality most obstacles stem from emotional roadblocks that we put there ourselves. Once we recognize them as objects that are approachable and able to be overcome, then we can begin to understand the ways around, over, or through the difficulty we believe is holding us back.

There are emotional bad-habit obstacles, as we've discussed in the sections above. Replacing negative statements with positive statements is one way to eliminate a specific bad-habit obstacle.

Other bad-habit obstacles are:

- not believing in your capabilities
- making assumptions about other people
- having an inaccurate or unrealistic definition of happiness or abundance
- underdreaming

What can you do to eliminate these bad-habit obstacles? First, you need to acknowledge that they exist. Then determine what will work for you to turn them into good habits.

Not Believing in Your Capabilities

The first one, not believing in your capabilities, can be resolved by the method discussed earlier in this chapter. Turning negatives into positives is the best way to do this. Identifying small successes related to your bigger choices will help toward believing in your own capabilities. For instance, if your goal is to become a world-renowned motivational speaker, you need to start small and gain some successes before you can be confident in your abilities, and build the credibility for others to hire you for bigger events.

Start by looking for opportunities to speak to local groups for business meetings. Many organizations, such as local Chambers of Commerce, Kiwanis clubs, Rotary organizations, and other clubs and associations enjoy speakers at their weekly or monthly club meetings. This is a great place to start. You write the speech, practice it a few times, preferably in front of people you trust or in front of a mirror, and change the things you don't like. Tape yourself if it helps you. Then you are ready to speak in front of a live group. And once you give a great presentation or speech, people who attended will want to recommend you to others they know who are looking for a speaker. Then you are on your way.

Assumptions

Making assumptions about others is a huge bad-habit obstacle. Many of us do this regularly, hardly realizing what it is we are doing to ourselves. We assume that someone will react or behave in a certain way in a certain situation. And then we act based on that assumption. We rarely reality-check our assumption to learn whether or not we were right.

When we do this, not only do we sell ourselves short, but we also disrespect the other person involved because, in effect, we made a decision for them. By not asking the question, "How would you feel if...?" or "What would you think about...?" or "Would you be willing to...?" we have presumed to know their mind better than they possibly could. How would you feel about someone making up your mind for you?

Inaccurate or Unrealistic Definitions

Determine whether what you want is something that can actually be attained. If your definition of abundance is something other than having more than enough, you should rethink your definition. If your idea of happiness is dependent upon someone other than yourself, perhaps you need to spend some time determining what you can do to create happiness in your life. Being happy is totally up to you, just as being successful is totally up to you, and having abundance is totally up to you. By continuing to blame others, or depend upon them for your happiness or success, you essentially give away the right to have what you want.

Underdreaming

In my experience, people underdream. Underdreaming is what we do when we allow ourselves to think about the positive "what if"—the dreams that we all have—and then sell ourselves short. What I mean by this is that we dream about what we want, but we don't dream big enough.

If you are going to dream, dream all the way! Think big and go after the things that you really, truly want—all of them—rather than limiting your dreaming because you think you couldn't possibly have all that!

As an example, when I made the choice to become a public speaker I could have limited my thinking, considering speaking before groups of 30 or 40 people at local clubs and organizations. As an author and trainer, there is probably sufficient business to make a living with that, and I would reach a fair number of people. If I limited myself to that line of thinking, would I be achieving my biggest dreams, or would I have been underdreaming?

In reality, when I chose to follow this path, my dreams consisted of speaking before audiences which numbered in the thousands. Why limit yourself? Dream BIG! If you are going to set a goal, why not set a big goal?

It makes logical sense to begin by speaking to smaller groups, and that is the path I followed. I still do. But today I also speak to very large groups, and am following my dream to get to as many people as I can, carrying the message that anyone can create the life they want.

As a society, we've been taught to be modest, not to be selfish, so we tend to not ask for all that we really want, in the hope of not seeming selfish to anyone else. Stop worrying about other people when you are dreaming YOUR dreams! Make a choice to dream BIG! By not dreaming about all of what you want, you limit your potential before you even get started.

Other methods that are useful in eliminating bad-habit obstacles include the following actions:

- Review your list of "Things at which I excel" regularly. Add to it whenever something comes to mind that isn't on that list. This provides a reminder about the "good stuff" so you can *feel* more successful, and therefore *be* more successful.

- Validate! Check into something you are unsure about. This is important in terms of assumptions, as discussed above, but is also important when it comes to information. Make sure you have the facts before you draw a conclusion. You may be placing obstacles in your own path because you think something is true and it isn't. Check the facts on anything that seems to be in the way of accomplishing your dreams.

- Put up positive affirmations where you will see them. And be aware when you encounter unbidden affirmations in your day-to-day experiences. A kind word about one of your goals; unexpected or unsolicited encouragement from someone; seeing something you've thought about in front of you in printed materials; coming across a poem, note, or section of scripture that is apropos to what you've been thinking about—all of these are affirmations that happen, as you will see when you begin to really pay attention to what happens around you.

- Ask another person to be your affirmation partner to alert you whenever you say something self-deprecating. This can be extremely powerful, especially for someone with low self-esteem. Being reminded regularly about how frequently you put yourself down can show very quickly the ways in which self-sabotage is rampant. If your self-esteem is solid and high, consider offering to do this for someone else. Either way, you win!

- Place a rubber band or string on your wrist to remind you to be positive about yourself, and to replace the negative thought with a positive thought.

Other Obstacles

There are personal obstacles that stem from severe personality issues. Because we are discussing obstacles, this needs to be identified as an obstacle. However, this book will not deal with overcoming these obstacle types, since the types of changes required are most often achieved only through therapeutic intervention by a mental health professional, such as a psychologist or psychiatrist.

The personal obstacles that require professional or medical intervention are those seen in people who have personality disorders, which can result in personality types like bullying, passive-aggressive personalities, or being so rigid in their thinking or belief system that they cannot function well in any relationship. Or, on the other hand, for an individual who has been so abused in his or her life that there is an insufficient sense of self to motivate, encourage, or build self-esteem, therapeutic intervention may be needed in order to succeed in making any life changes. This is by no means a complete list of the types of significant issues which may require professional intervention, but is intended to provide examples.

There are many personality types, as characterized by the mental health professionals, and this is not the forum in which to discuss the specific types of personality disorders or the related obstacles that people with personality disorders encounter. However, I would be remiss if I were not to mention that these issues do create obstacles, many of which are not easily overcome, and most of which will not be overcome using The CORE Approach™ alone.

Another type of obstacle is the reality-type obstacle, such as real people or setbacks, events, or situations that are outside of your control.

However real these obstacles may seem, they are frequently only perceived obstacles, and are not necessarily real. They may be formed from some of the emotional obstacles we identified earlier, but can arrive in our lives attached to real people or situations.

A primary obstacle of this type is one that involves family members or significant others. Frequently, the ones closest to us are the most resistant to the changes we want to make. It seems as though the opposite should happen, but in reality our loved ones are afraid that we will change and, as a result of that change, move away from them. This has more to do with them than us, but the behavior still represents an obstacle.

When encountering resistance from a significant other or family member, it helps to remember that people are often afraid of the unknown. Perhaps the person is concerned because he or she really doesn't understand the intended result for your change choice. In other words, "How will the fact that you are changing in this way affect me?" If you think about your intended audience when communicating about your choices and put yourself in his or her place, you will probably think of many of the concerns that person has about your changes. Talk about these assumptions or worries, and you will be that much closer to having a supportive partner or family member, rather than a resistant one.

We'll cover more ways to gain their support later on, but for now, just recognize that there are people in our lives who could be obstacles. The better you communicate with them about your goals, the more likely they are to get on board with your opportunity seeking and forward movement toward your goals.

Another reality-type obstacle is the belief that there isn't sufficient money to do what we want or need to do. There is always a certain element of risk in making changes. At times, we need to determine what temporary sacrifices need to be made in order to get past the obstacles and reach our goals. For many people, taking a financial risk is seen as such a large obstacle that they will not take that risk to make the changes, even though the changes would be ultimately beneficial to them, emotionally and financially.

A risk assessment needs to be done to determine whether the short-term risk outweighs the emotional or sacrificial discomfort that it may cause.

Financial independence is a common goal when discussing life changes, but few people actually achieve financial independence. Why do you think that is? It is possible to achieve financial independence, or abundance, so why do so few people get there?

Few people take a systematic look at their dreams. The CORE Approach™ suggests that you take a systematic view of your choices, goals, and dreams in order to determine what the risks are, whether or not the risks are acceptable ones, and develop ways to mitigate or eliminate those risks before they can become problems.

The elements of risk assessment are easy: identify the risk, determine the probability of the risk being real, identify ways that you can alleviate or minimize the risk, and monitor the risk for potential. These steps can be repeated as often as necessary until the risk is reduced or eliminated.

In regard to financial risk, there are numerous ways to obtain money needed for improving your life. I am sure this subject has been the subject of more than one book complete and separate from this book. If this is an issue for you, a trip to the local bookstore or library should help you find out more about ways to obtain the financing for your desired changes. A little research about credit cards, commercial lending, Small Business Association loans, grants, lines of credit based on equity, and other financing methods will help reduce the knowledge obstacle about this area.

When we think about the obstacle statements highlighted earlier, we see similarities. Let's review those statements:

- I couldn't do that — I don't have the_____ (experience, training, talent, etc.).
- I can't afford to leave my current job to make the changes I want to make.

- My (spouse, parents, children, etc.) won't understand.
- What if I try it and find out it's not what I want?
- People will think I'm crazy!
- If I did that, it would turn my family upside down.
- I'll be criticized for taking chances!
- What I want to do isn't what my degree is in—how will I have any credibility?
- What if it doesn't work out?
- I'll only be happy if I follow my dream of _____(art, social work, whatever your passion might be).
- I'll never have enough money to have a vacation home.

What do all of these statements have in common? One thing is that they are based on assumption, which as I mentioned, should be reality-checked rather than blindly accepted as true.

The more essential element is that they are based on needing something in order to move forward. Reassurance, affirmation, information or education, confidence, or a plan would alleviate all of these worries.

What causes worries and insecurities? I've spent an enormous amount of time thinking about this concept. What are the main things needed by people who want to make changes in their lives?

What will enable you to move over, through, or around the obstacles?

"Your silver shoes will carry you over the desert," replied Glinda. "If you had known their power you could have gone back to your Aunt Em the very first day you came to this country."

**Glinda, the Good Witch of the North, in
L. Frank Baum's *The Wonderful Wizard of Oz***

Chapter 4   Off to See the Wizard

The question posed at the end of the last chapter was:

> **What will enable you to move over, through, or
> around the obstacles?**

While thinking about it, in preparation for beginning this book, I was reminded of a spectacular story, written as a hobby by a salesman who liked to tell stories to children. The salesman was Lyman Frank Baum, and the story, *The Wonderful Wizard of Oz.* We'll actually talk more about Frank Baum's successes later—for now, I want to concentrate on the elements of the story itself.

Most people know the story of *The Wizard of Oz,* which was the movie title adapted from the original book. It is a story of a girl named Dorothy, from Kansas, whose house was lifted during a tornado and came to rest on an evil witch when it landed in Munchkinland, killing the witch. She awakens with a start, her dog Toto by her side, and is greeted by the Munchkinlanders, who bow to her, believing her to be a sorceress. She is celebrated as having saved them from the controlling reign of the Wicked Witch of the East. As a reward, she is given the witch's sparkling, and evidently powerful, magic shoes to wear, and told not to let them leave her feet.

Determined to return to Kansas, she is sent by her new friends along the Yellow Brick Road which leads to the Emerald City. She is assured she will be given the chance to meet the great Wizard of Oz there. It is this Wizard that they believe will enable her to travel back to Kansas.

Along the way she meets more new friends. Among these new friends are a scarecrow, a tin man, and a cowardly lion. Each of these characters also needs something, and they join Dorothy on her trek to the Emerald City to see if the Wizard will also help them.

What is it that Scarecrow, Tin Man and Lion are seeking, do you recall? Respectively, they are hoping to receive a brain, a heart and courage—right? And what is it that most people need in order to make the changes they want to make?

Knowledge, passion, courage.

If you have knowledge, passion, and courage, you can tackle anything and be successful. You actually can have one or two of these things and be successful, but with all three—with proper education, the courage to move ahead, and a path that is chosen straight from your heart, it's pretty tough to fail!

And what was it that Dorothy wanted? She wanted to go home. What did she have that eventually got her where she wanted to go? She had the gift of persistence. She just kept trying and trying, seeking opportunities and asking people, pushing for answers, finding ways to do what needed to get done in order to accomplish her goal. Eventually, she went home.

Yes, but…

Yes, but what about the obstacles? There were plenty of obstacles for Dorothy and her friends. First of all, no one she met had ever heard of Kansas, and consequently had no idea how to get her there.

Second, there was the problem of the witch killed by her falling house. This evil witch had a sister, who was pretty ticked off that Dorothy was the cause of her sister's demise. They encountered her a few times, and she represented the largest obstacle they had to face—even though the specific challenges were different each time they met her.

So, you are wondering, even if I have these three things—knowledge, passion, and courage—will there still be obstacles? My family might still be against the changes I want to make. My wife might not want me to change to a job where I won't make as much money until I get going.

Hang on—we'll get to that.

Let's go back to *The Wizard of Oz*. What is the biggest obstacle that Dorothy faces with Toto and her three newfound friends? Or, in literary terms, who is the antagonist in this story? She's the Wicked Witch of the West. What does the Wicked Witch represent? FEAR!

Fear is the underlying basis for obstacles. Back in the previous chapters, we discussed how fear shows itself in the obstacles you face. You may not think you are afraid, but if you boil down the obstacles, and truly evaluate all the thoughts, feelings, actions (or lack thereof), statements, and beliefs that accompany them, you will realize that there is fear underlying each roadblock.

You can face down the fear. Earlier chapters have presented you with a number of logical options to overcoming the fears. The reality check—learning all you can about the situation, and consequently eliminating the fear of the unknown, will move you farther along the success path than many other methods you may choose to try.

With *knowledge*, you will know how your family members feel about the changes you want to make. It might take courage to ask them, but once you do, you will know whether their reactions are really obstacles to be considered, or just fears fostered by your insecurity.

With knowledge, you will have the answers to the questions you may currently have about the ways in which to make your dreams come true. You can research financing options if you believe the obstacle is money. You can research different dieting and weight loss methods to find the one that suits your personality and motivation if you believe that you can't lose weight. You can research entrepreneurial options or job opportunities if your dream is to have a different career than you have now. The knowledge you gain will move you closer to believing that you can be successful and create the life you want!

"Yes, but how can I follow my dream if I don't know how to do what I want to do?"

Again, with knowledge you can handle anything that you need or want to do. It might mean more than just asking someone. It might require extensive research, taking classes, or even going back to school full time. Whether or not you can accomplish this depends on your level of passion about the change you want to make. If you are truly passionate about it, you will attain whatever knowledge you need not only move forward, but also to succeed beyond your wildest imagination.

Chances are you don't have all the knowledge you will need. You may or may not know how to get that knowledge. Again, this can cause fears and seem like an obstacle. Read on, and you'll learn some of the how-to's in this area.

Knowledge is power. It doesn't matter what knowledge it is—it's powerful somewhere in some circumstance. If you gain knowledge in the area of the changes you want to make, you will begin to become an expert and gain credibility. This will lead to self-esteem and a belief in your own abilities. The belief in yourself allows you to consider that you can, indeed, succeed. "I know I can succeed." See where this is going?

Remember—BIG dreams!

Passion. What are you passionate about? Chances are, it is contained on your "Things at which I excel" list. Spend some time considering what it is that really gets you going. What do you do, talk about, think about, or dream about that makes you feel excited and so full of joy to be alive that you think you might just burst. That is the element about which you are passionate.

If you have not felt that way about anything, spend some more time thinking about not only the things at which you excel, but list things you love. Perhaps you aren't a great musician, but you love music. Consider ways in which you can have a career in music without being a musician. There are a number of them, including such roles as producing concerts, conducting, being a musician's representative or a manufacturer's representative for musical instruments. When you begin to think creatively, the possibilities are almost endless.

You may not believe that your passion will be strong enough to see you through and be successful. "What if I'm not as passionate about this idea six months from now as I am now?" you might ask. (That, my friend, is a "what-if" question!) This is one of those areas requiring a lot of thought, research and time. Following your passion means paying attention to those feelings you've been pushing beneath the surface. Regardless of the situation, those just-beneath-the-surface feelings should gain your recognition. They mean something.

Passion is not a fleeting interest in the newest get-rich-quick scheme, no matter how strong a feeling it seems at the time. It is the feeling behind lifelong desires and long-term interests. It is rooted in the dreams you've always had, and have never let go. It is a feeling so powerful within you that you have never been able to completely ignore it. Pay attention to these desires.

The specifics of how your passion affects the changes you want to make may evolve. This is normal. When I started the training business, I thought that was my lone passion. What I determined as I worked through what this would take was that I really wanted to reach the individuals. I wanted to help people who wanted to pursue bettering their lives. It wasn't just about teaching corporate managers to be more effective managers and leaders, although I love doing that as well. I pursued corporate training, as planned, because of the revenue it would provide and the satisfaction I would get from knowing I was helping make the corporate world better. I also began to work through the plans for getting to an individual market for personal development—what I have found is an even stronger passion. It evolved. It's still evolving, and I'm excited about the next evolution and then the next one after that. Who knows what good things are still to come? Let it evolve.

What if...?

What if I can't resolve the obstacles? What if I can't get around them, through them, or over them? What if the fear is so great that I just can't see a way out?

Think about the Cowardly Lion for a minute. Do you remember the scene in the movie where he became quite scared because he thought someone was pulling his tail? Do you remember who was pulling his tail? Dorothy helped him discover that he was pulling his own tail.

We are frequently much like the Lion, pulling our own tails and not even realizing it. We create our own fears by dwelling on them, making them much bigger and more real than they need to be, and lending them credibility they don't really deserve.

You are more courageous than you know. What does this mean? Strength of character, assessment of risk and determining the level of acceptable risk, battling through odds that are stacked against us with knowledge and passion, identifying and breaking down obstacles, living through difficult times...all these things add to our courage.

Courage is built through proof. It is built by having successes. Courage is built by personal belief. Courage is built by persistence and perseverance. When our fears and obstacles come to the surface, courage helps us move past them. Sometimes fear holds us back—hopefully only temporarily. If we continue to move forward, recognizing the fear, and knowing that the risk is minimal or at an acceptable level, that's courage.

I've learned from life that we are all significantly stronger than we believe ourselves to be. This is especially true when it comes to something about which we are passionate. Consider what you would do—how strong you could be—if someone you loved were in danger. What would you do to get that loved one away from the danger? Where there is passion, there is strength of conviction. Courage.

Give up the fear.

Figure out where the fear comes from, wallow in it for a time if you must, and then make a conscious choice to give it up. The Lion allowed himself to be convinced that the fear was neurotic and he became less frightened being with his friends. By searching for the sources that create the fear, and by believing in your passion and being on the right path, the fear will decrease and your confidence will increase.

> **What if I still can't achieve my chosen changes, even if I feel like I'm doing all the right things? I've learned what I need to know; I'm following a path that is created by my passion; and I'm doing my utmost to have the courage to move forward. Now what?**

The answer to these questions depends largely on how you have been raised and what you were taught. There is one more element that Dorothy had in her repertoire—perseverance. She was bound and determined to get back to Kansas, witch or no witch. Her passion fueled her determination and perseverance.

Personally, I've always believed that I could accomplish whatever I set out to do. Someone recently asked me why I believe that, and my answer was that it never occurred to me that I would fail.

Experience has taught me that there are always answers to perceived problems, if you want to find those answers. Through research, investigation, education, perseverance, common sense, confidence, and sometimes even trial and error, people can accomplish just about anything. It takes believing, knowing, moving through the fear when it surfaces, and continuing to be passionate about the dream as well as the results.

If Dorothy and her friends hadn't persevered, they would never have gotten to the Emerald City and gained an audience with the "great and powerful wizard." If they had given up, who knows where they might have ended up? Even though the Wicked Witch of the West kept cackling at them, writing threats in the sky, sending winged monkeys after them, and casting spells on them, they continued to believe in their purpose of getting to the Wizard to seek their true desires.

Let's try something.

Get out your notebook—the one where you've been keeping your lists. In your notebook, write one obstacle statement on each page and beneath it write all the reasons you consider it to be an obstacle. Keep asking yourself "why" or "why not" after each statement, and eventually, you will get to the fear base.

When you've finished, you'll have a list of fears. Chances are, the list will boil down to one or two fears that you'll recognize.

In the box, you will find an example. Once you have reviewed this sample exercise, try some examples from your own list.

Obstacle: My wife will think I'm crazy if I go home and tell her I've been thinking about quitting my decent-paying job and want to start my own retail business.

Why: She knows me as someone who doesn't make quick or frivolous decisions.

Why not: I am always the one who is strong and stable, considering all angles before I make changes or decisions.

Why: That's the way I've always been.

Why:	I was taught that the man's role is to always been the breadwinner and the source of stability for the family.
Why:	That's the way my family did it. That's the way it should be.
Why:	Because I'm the strong one.
Why:	Because that's the way she sees me, even if it's not always true.
Why not:	I'm not always as strong as I let her believe.
Fear:	My wife won't see me as strong anymore, and maybe she won't love me.

Do you see how this exercise works? Continue to question your belief statements until you get to the place where you absolutely have to be honest with yourself, in order to understand the underlying fear. Trust me, it is always there—you just need to be willing to recognize some things about yourself that may not be the most pleasant to think about. If you allow yourself to be honest, you will make a lot of progress toward eliminating fear from your life.

One of the biggest fears we all have—hence an obstacle—is the fear of what others will think. Fear of criticism. We are frequently afraid of what others will think or believe—or worse, what they will say to us. Criticism never has a positive connotation. It is always considered negative. However, viewed in the right light, and used correctly, criticism can be very helpful.

I believe one man summed up the answer to this fear quite well:

> *"If you are not criticized, you may not be doing much."*
>
> **Donald H. Rumsfeld (1932-)**
> **Secretary of Defense, United States of America**

Criticism is an excellent indicator that you are moving forward. It is proof that you are doing something—taking action. Consider the positive outcomes of having to deal with criticism from others. Frequently, the criticism is stemming from the other person's fear that somehow through what you are doing, something will change for them. Again, this is fear of the unknown. Consider it their obstacle, not yours, and you will be healthier and more courageous.

We all need to get past the fears that we carry as our baggage in order to get to the Wizard. The goal is to get to the Wizard— whatever YOUR Wizard is—obtaining the knowledge, passion, and courage along the way that you need to live your dream. Then persevering with smaller obstacles and using the process in order to go for the BIG dream.

Once we realize what this is—that all these obstacles are based in fear—then we can figure out how to get rid of the witch and get what we need. Fear is so incapacitating that we may not believe we can still learn, have enough passion, or show the courage to create the life we want.

Knowledge, passion. And courage.

Courage. What if...we just aren't brave enough to weather the storms or rocky seas that come our way on this chosen path? What if...we don't have the courage to see it through? Or the perseverance? What if...we don't have sufficient strength?

There are a lot of "yes, but..." and "what if..." statements and questions when you deal with the subject of change. Any "what if" or "yes, but" statements are negative statements. See if you can change them into positive statements. Try to turn them into statements such as "However, if we considered...then we could..."

Perhaps these statements, turned to a positive perspective from a negative stance, could lead to the next iteration of a phenomenal concept or idea. Just think of the endless possibilities if we were all positive about our abilities and capacity all the time!

The interesting thing about the story of Dorothy and *The Wizard of Oz* is the fact that Dorothy had the power to go home all along. Think about that. How powerful would you be if you believed—if you really *knew*—that you have the power to succeed within you right now?

What could you accomplish? How many others could you help? What would you build, create, or develop? What goals could you reach? How far could you go? Would your achievements exceed your wildest imagination? Would you be able to stop under-dreaming, and dream BIG?

You have the power within you right now to achieve whatever you choose, and create the life you want.

There are three questions to be answered before moving into the creative phase of your changes:

> **Do I have the knowledge I need?**
>
> **What is my passion?**
>
> **How strong is my courage?**

"Most folks are about as happy as they make up their minds to be."
Abraham Lincoln (1809-1865)

Chapter 5   Why Can't I Just Be Happy?

Just think—if I had the answer to this question, I'd be the wealthiest person on earth!

Most people feel this way at times. Usually, the feeling passes after a short time as we receive reminders about how fortunate we are and how much we really do have. Think about what you already know you have—love from your families, talent that you use to make money, or other blessings for which you are grateful.

But then the feeling surfaces again, and again, and again.

**Why am I not happy with my life?
Why can't I just be content with the
way things are?**

Why *can't* we just be happy? We cannot be happy because society teaches us not to be satisfied.

First, we live in a constant state of bigger, better, faster. The twentieth century saw so many technological advances that the current generation and those coming up behind us are constantly bombarded with ways to get information, food, and whatever else we need quicker than ever before. Bandwidth for getting to the Internet is becoming more and more available, thus making our access faster all the time.

Ask a 15 year old about getting to the Internet on dial-up and they think you live in the dark ages. And there are still plenty of households that either don't have high speed access to the Internet, don't have access at all, or don't have a computer, or perhaps even a television or telephone! But, once we do have those things, we want the next better thing, don't we?

We live in the era of fast. Fast response on our computers. Information at our fingertips via the Internet or the television remote control. Fast food via the drive-through lane or pre-cooked food heated in the microwave oven. Fast.

There are while-you-wait oil changes for the car, shoe repair, online libraries and reference materials for research, online banking. Fast.

We don't have to go out to shop. Mail order catalogs with toll-free numbers and online shopping have made it all easy-access. We can even get faster delivery just by paying a fee for premium delivery service. Fast.

We're in the society of instant gratification. It's all about FAST.

And we wonder why we aren't content? What does the age of instant gratification say about our relationships with others?

We treat our relationships as though they are FAST-driven, too. This includes our personal relationships as well as our business and co-working relationships. We want what we want immediately. We tend to be a "me-first" society. Although I don't advocate it, living me-first for some period of time does seem to be the catalyst toward the "getting back to basics" trend that we are beginning to see. The positive outcome is that more and more people are evaluating what is important to them and to their families. For some, this means living more simply, with less physical, emotional, and calendar clutter. For others, this means finding something to do for a living that has meaning to them, something that is not just a job and a paycheck.

Many people are seeking life work that uses their talents, or that enables them to help others. Some want to have a better balance between their work life and their home life.

More and more people are giving up that climb to the top of the corporate ladder. Personally, this was the crux of the problem for me. Although I was in a career I liked, and by all accounts was more than proficient, I was becoming increasingly frustrated about the politics and lack of values I was witnessing in corporate America. The emphasis on the dollars and cents outweighed the emphasis on the human assets (the people!) and this didn't sit right with me. The "cents" overpowered "sense."

And I wasn't happy. Don't get me wrong—there was a lot that was perfect in my life. I was blessed with a good job, a wonderful husband, kids that were good kids by most people's standards, and quite a comfortable life. But something was missing. It's a sort of empty feeling—not always easy to label. Identifying what was missing was the key.

I'm a strong-willed, determined, assertive-bordering-on-aggressive, and sometimes stubborn, woman. People who know me will tell you that I generally get what I want. But what some people don't know about me is that I spend a lot of time thinking about, praying about, and assessing the "rightness" of what I think I want before I make a decision about it. And, at times, what I thought I wanted has turned out not to be what I wanted at all! I'm not alone here, am I?

I'm also someone who genuinely cares for people. I want everyone to have abundance in their life in whatever way is meaningful for them. So, for me, the leap away from corporate America had to include a way to help others reach decisions for what they want to change in their lives, and provide for them a way to make those changes. Of course, this wasn't crystal clear at first, and there are still times I revise courses and chapter texts that I've written as new experiences teach me even more.

The position I held was lucrative. Certainly, I was satisfied with the salary and bonus I was receiving. Money was not the motivator for my leap of faith. I needed to make major changes in my life, and in turn, that of my family.

No, the motivator wasn't money. It was the knowledge that I had more to offer, that I wasn't using my God-given talents in ways that excited me. I wasn't making a difference. Following my passion for teaching was the primary motivating factor.

I knew I had something to pass on that could help some people. I had been a trainer in many areas of my career, so it was something I knew. This led to a decision to create a training and development company. Was this what was going to make me happy? At that point I didn't know, so I had to do some research, some soul searching, a lot of questioning whether or not I was on the right path for my life, quite a bit of praying, and a LOT of discussing with my husband, who wasn't so sure he wanted our household income cut almost in half while I started a business!

First things first—what obstacles was I facing?

We talked earlier about knowledge, passion, and courage. As an example, I can use my own experience to illustrate how knowledge, or lack of it, can be an obstacle or simply an observation of something missing in your resources.

I had owned my own business earlier in my career, but not a training company. I had been a sole proprietor previously, not a corporation, and I had no employees in the earlier experience. There were some things to be learned. So, I needed knowledge. But not having sufficient knowledge was not an obstacle for me, because I have always believed that I could gain the knowledge I needed.

This is one key to understanding your success capability. Lack of knowledge should not be considered an obstacle. If you can learn, you can gain the knowledge you need. It does not always have to be something you start with. It helps to have a general knowledge of the area in which you want to follow your dream, but specific knowledge can be gained as you research and move forward toward your goals.

Did I have the passion to do this? The passion came from a variety of areas. It came from the desire to create something that would help others in many ways. It came from the desire to be my own boss with my own schedule, so that I could be more available to my family. It came from part of my character that is creative and loves the challenge of building new things. And it came from a desire for financial independence—a desire whose roots were fear.

As another example from my own experience, the fear of not having enough money can be monumental. There were plenty of times in my life when money was a struggle and a constant worry. There were times when I'd buy frozen food because I felt that if there was food in the freezer, there wouldn't be hunger in the house. There were times as a single mother when I had to swallow my pride and ask my ex-husband to help by buying winter coats for our children, even though he was paying child support, because there just wasn't enough money for all that they needed.

The fear I had was that I would not be able to provide for my family. To alleviate that fear, my choice (my decision) was to find a better job that would use more of my skills and pay a higher salary.

This is just one example of how something negative—a strong fear—can be turned into a positive. In more recent years, I made a choice to have financial independence as a goal, rather than let that old fear engulf me and keep me stuck in a good job. Sounds funny, huh? "...stuck in a good job." It is funny, but a good job wasn't going to get me financial independence. Financial independence is part of my passion.

It may sound as if I'm being greedy when I speak of wanting financial independence, but in reality some of the desire comes from wanting to be able to help others in a more significant manner than I could with the level of income I had at the time. If I were to become financially independent, I could participate in a Habitat for Humanity day or week without worrying about getting paid that day or that week. If I were to become financially independent, I could put together fund-raising events for charity and not need to worry about whether I had vacation time to cover the days off I would need. If I were to become financially independent, some worries for my family would be alleviated. And so on. These were my thoughts at the time.

Passion. Did I have the passion to move forward with my goals? Absolutely!

Courage, now there's another story. It's hard to have courage all the time. No matter how strong you are, or what you've been through in your life—the "yes, but..." and "what if..." fears come through. This is my constant struggle. I've managed to repeat enough positive affirmations, enlist support from those around me, and succeed enough to be brave more and more. But, as I said, this is a constant struggle. Hopefully, it won't be yours!

So, we've covered the knowledge, passion and courage obstacles. And believe me, it took quite a while to be able to visualize and verbalize them this concisely.

Next steps: What were the reality obstacles? There were quite a number of them, as I recall.

- My husband was not at all sure that he was pleased with this discovery I had made about myself. I thought that his reaction and his lack of comfort about the changes to our financial position, however temporary, was an obstacle.

- Financial adjustments would have to be made. Were we willing to sacrifice a fairly comfortable lifestyle, with our oldest in college, and three more coming up behind him? Not to mention the orthodontia bills, dances, class trips, music lessons, basketball league fees (and shoes for quickly growing teenage feet!) and any number of luxury expenses that had become the norm for us.

- There would be schedule changes for the family—big ones, especially since I'd be working at home, but would also have to travel at times. Some of these, like being home more were considered good (by me) and bad (by the kids).

- Did I have the self-discipline to work at home full-time? I had worked at home part-time in other roles where I did not have to be in the office all the time, but now I'd be considering being at my home office full-time. Did I really have the discipline to ensure that I hit my goals each week, and not spend the time redecorating the house?

- I would be working primarily alone for some period of time until the business reached a size appropriate to hire staff. This would be different for me. Would I miss having someone at the office with whom to discuss things, use as a sounding board, confidant, or humor outlet?

- What resources would I need, and did I have them? By going into business for myself, I'd be giving up my corporate-loaned computer and have to buy a laptop, printer, and make some other investments.

- Who would my human resources be? Who would be my dream team, the people I would depend on for support and advice?

There were other considerations, but this list shows the majority of the larger obstacles. As I look back, I can identify and enumerate these obstacles clearly, but there were moments, even after the choices and decisions were made, that I was completely paralyzed.

This process to approaching change is not a once and done, or an all or nothing process. There are times in even the most productive weeks, such as the weeks in which large contracts are signed for business deals, when the doubts still arise and need to be pushed away. This was more frequent in the early weeks and months, but this still happens at times.

These are examples of the temporary obstacles that fear causes. And for me, this is where faith plays a big part. If I've been led to this choice I've made, and continue to believe I am on the right path, it is easier to push those fears aside, even if they won't go away completely. It is simpler to just acknowledge that they are there, but not give in to them, and simply know that my path has not diverged, that we're still in the building phase — and we will constantly be in the building phase, so these types of fears will continue to surface.

This is also where perseverance comes into play. Continuing along the chosen path, while assessing and reassessing the opportunities to achieve the chosen goals, is an act of faith in what you are doing that requires courage and perseverance to continue despite difficulties or worries.

This has been an awfully long answer to the question of "Why can't I just be happy?" I wanted to illustrate to you that our life circumstances can be quite happy and something can still be missing, if we aren't following our hearts. The passion—the heart—of our calling, if you will, is what makes life fulfilling.

My friend John Strelecky, in his book *The Why Are You Here Café*, calls it your Purpose For Existing. If you haven't read John's book, and you still don't know your true passion, pick up a copy and spend the short time it will take to read through the book. You might be surprised by the huge impact such a seemingly small book can have.

What is your heart telling you? Are you listening? Sometimes it comes as a still, small voice, a gentle nagging that you push away over and over again, until eventually it refuses to be ignored or pushed away. Other times it resounds like a big brass band, and all at once you know what it is that's been missing.

Once you begin to think about these things, if you are aware of your surroundings, you will begin to get messages. They won't always be spoken words, and I'm not suggesting that you will hallucinate, but there will be times that someone will say exactly what you were thinking about. Or you will read an article about whatever change-oriented subject you were thinking about. Or someone will give you a book, send you a quote, or mention someone they know, and it will be related to your thoughts about this change.

If you are not sure what will provide a more fulfilling life for you, ask. Ask yourself, ask your higher power, ask the universe, or ask your spouse or best friend. You may be surprised by the answers you get.

There are two cautionary statements I want to make to you about asking for answers:

1.   Make sure you are paying attention for the answers. They won't always come to you in conventional ways.

2.   Don't ask friends and relatives if you aren't willing to consider their answers with credibility. They may provide you with answers that you dislike, or that are completely different from the path you were considering. Think about their answers before you discard them, or before you judge them not to be credible. My first book idea came from my husband, and I wasn't even thinking along the lines of the idea he presented. Sometimes the people close to us know us better than we know ourselves.

What makes your life fulfilling will be different from what makes others' lives work for them. Only you can make the choices and decisions that will set you on the path to *Change Your Life!* and create the life you want.

"The strongest principle of growth lies in human choice."

George Eliot (1819-1880)
Author, *Middlemarch*, and other works
Pen-name of Mary Ann Evans

Chapter 6   The CORE of the Matter

What is The CORE Approach™? It is a four step methodology that takes you through the necessary thought processes and actions to make changes in your life. It is conceptually simple, but is rather difficult to integrate into your personality or character.

When I started the training business a couple of years back, a number of people told me that they could not have done what I did. When I asked why, they had various reasons, most of which stemmed from their fears. These conversations made me think about the "how" of what I had done. I knew why, but I had never analyzed how I had done it. The result of my analysis is The CORE Approach™.

CORE is an acronym for Choice, Opportunity, Responsibility and Expectation. In a very condensed form, it is about making conscious choices, seeking out and being aware of opportunities that will move you further toward your choices, being responsible and giving back in some manner, and setting your internal expectations appropriately, thus allowing others to have the proper expectation of you and your actions.

The CORE Approach™ was developed because I was seeking a systematic method to teach to people who wanted to make changes in their lives, but were stuck. I had been there. Being stuck is not fun. When you're stuck, you usually don't know how to get unstuck.

It took me quite some time to move forward with the changes I wanted to make. Even after beginning to make the changes, although I always had the passion, there were times when I had insufficient knowledge, resources, or courage to keep moving forward.

The process of getting through all of the obstacles—my obstacles—was the basis for The CORE Approach™. I thought about the process that helped me through it all, and how I could reduce it to a simple, easy-to-follow formula. I wanted to help others make changes without the anguish that I experienced.

It all starts with a choice.

CHOICE

First, I made choices about my life. We all have choices to make each and every day. We choose what to wear, our food and what time our meals will be, what we will do each day, and much more. Most of us go through our lives with these relatively unconscious choices happening all the time. But what about the big stuff?

The choices I made were about the big stuff. These were conscious choices about what I wanted to do for a living and how I wanted my life to be structured. They were choices based on what I was truly passionate about in this life. I made a choice to stop working in corporate America, even though I had achieved a position of status with a solid, six-figure salary.

I made a choice to start a business. I made a choice to be more available to my teenage children, through flexible hours and working from my home.

Did I know if any of it would work? Not at that point. But you know, it also never occurred to me that I would fail. I had to start somewhere, with a conscious choice, and a positive attitude. If you don't start, and you don't have a positive attitude, you don't get very far at all.

As I said, the first choice I made was to choose a different career path that would provide me with the fulfillment I was seeking.

Over the years, I spent a lot of time working on my personality and my character. I often wondered if other people regularly do this, or whether I was part of an insightful group of colleagues at an earlier part of my career that proved to be a blessing for me.

In evaluating myself and through listening to others' feedback, I learned that I needed to actively listen and not interrupt others. I learned that my integrity was important and that I always needed to do what I said I would do when I said I would do it. Truth had always been important to me, but over time, it became the only way.

There were other things I worked on as well, but the point here is that I had to make choices about who I was going to be, and how I was going to be that person. The big things were pretty easy, but some of the smaller, yet still important, character traits were more difficult to attain. Things like choosing to smile, being positive, and being peaceful, regardless of the situation. These things included choosing the right attitude for success. As some of you know, I'm still working on some of these, especially the "always peaceful" one!

Choices are not always easy to stick by once we make them. If they are important enough, we manage to find a way, but sometimes there's a trade-off or a sacrifice.

The fulfillment I wanted and needed was in doing work that would help others. I love being a trainer—being in front of a group and instigating a lively discussion about some topic or another. Training had been part of my career path, so I had some knowledge about it as I began putting this company together in my mind.

In addition, there were several people I could call on as resources to be my team of experts. And there were those with whom I had worked who wanted to work together again, so getting good people wouldn't be too much of a problem.

I was going to have to make some difficult choices about some other things, like developing the marketing campaign, using outside help for things I didn't know enough about, and other details, but they weren't part of the initial choice. They came later.

The fulfillment I wanted and needed also included having a schedule that would allow me to be at home more frequently and be a bigger part of my teenagers' lives. The fears a mother faces when she has teenagers are monumental compared to any fear related to a career change!

One of my choices about this career change was that I would work more flexible and fewer hours. A current goal is not to work on Fridays, or at least work at home on Fridays, and not for the entire day. So far, I've been successful at meeting this goal about 90% of the time. A future goal is to take off one week each month. I think that one will take a while longer.

For me, the major choices were relatively easy, because I knew what I loved and what I wanted to do. If your choices are not so clear-cut, begin by thinking about where your passions lie, and what changes you could make that would incorporate some things about which you are passionate. It's the "Do What You Love" philosophy.

Other changes, such as character style improvements may be even more difficult. None of us likes to acknowledge that we aren't perfect. The sooner you can acknowledge negative patterns that need to be changed, or traits that you admire about another person and would like to have within yourself, the sooner you can be on the road to having the life you want.

What choices do you want or need to make for yourself?

OPPORTUNITY

Now that my choices were made, I needed to know if there were opportunities to have this life I wanted. I found out that opportunities are all around you if you look for them, and if you are open to them.

It's funny about opportunities. We seem to want them to show up in just the way that we expect. First of all, they don't always just "show up." Often it takes effort and creativity to proactively seek an opportunity to move closer toward one of our choices.

Second, there are times when we think we don't have opportunities, but in reality, they are before us. What happens is that our expectations get in the way. What I mean by this is that we are not always open to accepting opportunities in any way that they might be presented to us. We expect to have something happen in a certain manner or form, and we miss an opportunity altogether because we were not open to receiving some event or action as an opportunity. We did not view it in that perspective, and therefore missed it. This happens more often than you might think.

For instance, when I incorporated the training business, I thought I had left the information technology field. The service offerings were oriented mostly toward managerial skills development and leadership. One day when I was struggling to understand where the next revenue was going to come from, my husband called and told me that an old friend and colleague had called him to get my number.

As it turned out, the friend did call, and it was a very lucrative conversation. I never expected the call to be business related because he and I had worked together in an information technology firm, and I wasn't doing information technology training (or so I thought). This conversation proved to be the lead-in to a joint sales call and a very productive training engagement with a Fortune 500 client!

As I said, I never expected that this would be an opportunity to further the business, but since I was open to it, it resulted in increased business revenue and an impressive client on the client reference list.

When I think back to the first thoughts about having my own business, and the opportunities, I knew I had several. There were a number of ways I could work more flexible hours, and there were plenty of businesses I could start. What I needed to know were things like what the costs were going to be to get started, what help I would need and have, whether I wanted or needed a partner or investor, how I would get clients, and all the personal opportunities that went with this decision. The personal opportunities included things like finding support, guidance, cheerleading, mentoring, and help around the house when I was working, in addition to identifying the ways in which I could give to others.

I was able to reinforce in my own mind the concept that not only did I have to view each and every conversation, chance meeting, discussion in a grocery store line, and networking event as an opportunity, but I also needed to stay open to the possibility that things I never considered to be business related could also be opportunities. Now, whenever something unexpected happens, rather than being thrown off, I think about what I'm supposed to learn from the change, or how I should use it as an opportunity to further my goals. This is starting to become second nature to me, but it has taken quite some time for that to happen, and it is by no means always present. It is not easy to condition yourself to think of everything you do as an opportunity to further your goals.

Considering that the business has been around a while now, that a second entity has been formed, and that my family has not fallen apart, it seems that I found many of the opportunities that were presented to me or that I sought, and life is good! I can only wonder which ones I missed.

What opportunities do you need to seek out or recognize to take you to your choices?

RESPONSIBILITY

Having made these choices, and having begun to be creative in my thinking about opportunities, a funny thing happened. I couldn't get rid of the restless sense of "service" inside myself. I suppose that sounds cryptic, but it isn't meant to be.

Many people find themselves with a restless or empty feeling, frequently described as a strange feeling in the pit of the stomach. Perhaps you have felt this as an anxious feeling. I felt it in my gut, physically, and knew that something still wasn't right. I was actually beginning to feel guilty. I had everyone's support in leaving my full-time employed position, starting my business, and beginning to create the life I'd dreamed about, and I still wasn't happy. What was wrong?

I was going to help people. I was going to "give back." But it wasn't feeling quite right yet.

Giving back was one of the main reasons I had wanted to start the business. So, the next thing I had to do was determine all the ways I could help others. What was to be my responsibility after making these choices and seeking these opportunities?

I believe that we get back in multiples of what we give, especially when we give from the heart, with no intention of gaining. We are each responsible to be in service of some type, often several types of service, throughout our lives.

One choice was easy—I would be responsible to anyone who worked for or with me, to provide to them what they required in order to spend the time with me and with the business. In other words, I assumed a responsibility to be a premier employer.

But I also knew that I have an ongoing responsibility to give back to the world at large. We all do. So, even though we weren't making any money yet, in the first year I organized and ran a charity event for a local food kitchen and my church's women's group charity. It was additional cost in dollars and time, but it was something I just knew I had to do. Don't get me wrong—I wanted to do it, and I knew the publicity wouldn't hurt at all—but I also knew that I **had** to do it. I knew because of the way the idea felt, and then grew when I put it out to a few people. I knew by the enthusiasm the idea generated in those it would benefit as well as those who participated.

The event was successful, although with a limited time frame in which to advertise, it was not as successful as I would have preferred. What I found in this "giving" were opportunities for recognition in the community, additional friendships and business relationships, credibility, and good will.

So much good will was generated that I've gotten referrals from some of the relationships that developed. In addition, on the Friday following the event, a lucrative contract came to me, seemingly from nowhere. When you give, it always comes back to you. Perhaps not immediately, and not always in ways you might expect, but it does come back to you.

How will your responsibility be reflected in the choices you make and the opportunities you seek? Where and how will you give back?

EXPECTATION

Having ideas, making conscious choices, being open and proactive about opportunities, and being responsible were all good things. This concept began to seem as though it did, in fact, have clear steps to it. But again, I continued to feel as if it wasn't complete. Something was still missing.

Let's get back to the question of what had to be done in order to make the career change I was seeking. I had done all the right stuff, at least in my own mind. I finally realized that the last thing I had to do was confirm my internal expectations. What did I expect all this to yield? What were my expectations of myself in regard to capability and success? And what expectations would I have to set for others around me? Who were the others that I had to consider?

My own expectations should be easy to categorize. Or so I thought. I knew that I expected the best of myself all the time. Not too much to ask, is it? Maybe it's not too much to ask, but it's awfully difficult to live up to. Thus began the self-dialogue that ensued for weeks.

What did I expect? Certainly, I expected to succeed. I always expect to succeed or I don't undertake whatever it is that I believe won't succeed at that time. But what defined success for this venture? Success is a relative term. I still needed to work on that part of the expectation.

What else did I expect? I expected that everyone around me would be as excited as I was about these changes. Now, talk about unrealistic expectations…! Not only was my family not excited, they weren't even a little bit enthusiastic. I had some expectation setting work to do there.

Business associates and colleagues, however, were impressed with the ideas I was presenting and reinforced and affirmed my belief that success was possible. In fact, for a period of about three months, I received affirmation after affirmation, in many and varied ways, that I was clearly on the right track.

Aside from success, what else did I expect? I expected to work hard to get the business off the ground, and that there would be a lot to do myself. Finally—a realistic expectation. Not to mention the *understatement* of the year.

I expected business to come in sooner and in a different manner than it did. I expected to be farther along in the development and production process than I ever was at the appointed milestone date. I expected to have more help than I had. As you might see in this potential pattern, there were a number of expectations I held which proved to have a different outcome than my original expectation. However, with all expectations, flexibility is the key, as well as a willingness to understand why something turns out differently than you might have expected. This is part of the learning process in setting appropriate internal (self) and external (others') expectations.

In retrospect, you can often see where your expectation setting was flawed and avoid disappointment or failure in the future. Use this clear hindsight as a learning process in order to be more efficient at building successes. These success stories will enhance expectations for the future. Being open and insightful, with a willingness to be creative, will enable the expectation process in The CORE Approach™ to become a natural part of your personality.

These are the basic premises of The CORE Approach™. As you can see, this is a system of simple concepts which is complicated by the complexity of our lives. Four steps—Choice, Opportunity, Responsibility, Expectations. Each of these steps is an entity unto itself. Each one takes thought, process, research, intellect, awareness, and action in order to be fully useful in working through changes.

You can certainly be successful using some combination of the four concepts—using some but not others. But will you have abundance in all areas of your life? Will you reap rewards for body, mind, and soul? Combining the individual concepts of Choice, Opportunity, Responsibility and Expectation—indeed, using The CORE Approach™—provides a powerful tool for creating the life you want.

"It's choice—not chance—that determines your destiny."

Jean Nidetch
Founder of Weight Watchers

Chapter 7   Choice

Life comes with choices.

What we do with them determines not only what we can achieve, but also who we become. What we do with them determines whether we live an intentional life, or whether we just take things as they come to us.

Which do you think is better? Going through life accepting what comes your way? Or living an intentional life, by making conscious choices and good decisions?

Many of us have let life happen to us, rather than making the life we want. Is this you? For a long time, it certainly was the way I lived my life.

There are people who don't recognize the choices they have. This could be for a variety of reasons. Perhaps they were convinced early in their lives that they didn't have choices. Perhaps they weren't given the tools to make good choices, and as a result have learned that making choices is a bad thing. Perhaps after having made some bad choices for themselves, they've lost the ability to believe that they can make good choices. Whatever the reason, many people are unaware of the choices that exist for them. The first choice, when you seriously want to make changes, and live an intentional life, is to be conscious about the choices that exist around you.

> **Choice #1:** *Choose to make choices.*
> *Make good ones.*

Most of us would like to make some changes and improvements in our lives. But we all know that change can be extremely difficult, even if we take small steps toward our goal. Sometimes the difficulty is in finding the right goal to begin with.

What is it that you want to change? What choices do you have in regard to that desired change? Which of those choices are good choices?

Think about the times in your life in which you have made conscious choices about something important. How many can you recount?

If you are fortunate, you will have a number of items on your list of important life paths in which you have made conscious choices.

The more likely scenario is that you will quickly realize that many of your life paths have been determined by chance or by going with the flow of events that have transpired in your life. These paths were followed without conscious choice.

> **Choice #2:** *Choose your values.*

If I were to ask you to describe the values on which your life is based, would that be an easy task? Have you ever thought about what your values really are?

What do I mean by *values*? There are several dictionary definitions for values because the word can be used in many different ways in the English language. The definition to which I refer in this section is, according to *The Illustrated Oxford Dictionary*, "one's principles or standards; one's judgment of what is valuable or important in life."

Using that definition, can you now answer the question, "What are the values on which your life is based?"

I can tell you that the values on which my life is based include integrity, truth, excellence, and divine illumination. I can also tell you that I did not arrive at these values as the answer to that question quickly or without insightful struggle. It takes a lot of thoughtful, introspective probing to come up with even one or two real core values.

The questions to ask are:

- ✔ What values are most important to me?
- ✔ What values do I want others to see in me?
- ✔ What values do I seek in my relationships?

What words come immediately to your mind? Take the time to write them down. They're probably pretty close to being your basic values. After learning more, you might just need to refine them slightly to fit your personality or goals.

Values can be defined by many nouns, such as the ones I've chosen—integrity, truth, excellence, and divine illumination, as well as faith, service, love, respect, dignity, safety, equality, justice, humility, charity, honor, and countless others.

You'll notice that I included all positive words. There are also many negative words that represent values. Hatred, power, conflict, pain, negativity, emotionalism, pride, fear, and inconsistency would all be considered negative values.

The point here is to make positive changes in your life. If the values on which your life is based are negative, you'll have to think long and hard about Choice #2—Choose Your Values. Choosing to change your basic values from negative values to positive values could be a difficult process.

Choosing your values may be second nature. They may already be inherent in you, and you just need to name them. If not, take a look at people you admire, whether or not they are people you know. Think about family, celebrities, mentors, teachers, and others who may have had an influence in your life. What traits do they have that cause you to respect them? Chances are, these are also the traits that you have already, or that you desire to have as your values. For instance, if you admire truthfulness, but have a tendency to stretch the truth a bit, this is one area you can choose to work on. Adopt truth as a basic value and consciously work on telling the truth at all times.

If you are still struggling with what to call the values on which you base your life (or want to base your life in the future), think about the following:

- What impression do I want to leave with others?
- How do I want to be remembered?
- What legacy do I want to create?
- What types of relationships do I want to have?

The answers to these questions will help you identify the character you want to have and project to others. As you answer these questions, think about the words that come to mind. Write them down. Continue to work on this process over a period of days, or even weeks. It might not be readily obvious if you have never thought about these things before reading this book.

Choose three basic values that resonate with you. Work on those three, and any related values they may have. For instance, if one of the values you feel you have is service, then helpfulness, charity, and kindness might all be related values. Keep a journal of these ideas until you have it narrowed down to three that feel right.

By now you've chosen to make choices, rather than just accepting what life drops in your lap. You're also at some point along the road of determining the basic values by which you want to live the rest of your life. What's next?

Choice #3: *Choose your goals.*

Now, make choices about your goals. What do you want from the rest of your life? What do you want to do? Where do you want to go? What do you want to see? Who do you want to meet? What does success look like to you, in terms of your family, your career, your relationships, your wealth, your attitudes, your health, and your appearance? Which things are really important to you?

Mark Victor Hansen, co-author of the multimillion dollar best-selling *Chicken Soup for the Soul* books, suggests writing 101 goals in a notebook. Use the questions in the previous paragraph to spark the thought process. It might seem a daunting task to come up with over 100 goals, but once you get started, it gets easier. Things you see and do during your day-to-day activities spark ideas about things you want to do that you then add to the list.

Start with the big things. Then think about the smaller ones. The big things could be physically or emotionally driven, and could be relatively easy to achieve, or very difficult.

For instance, say your first goal is to go to Hawaii someday. If you are healthy, there should be no physical reason why you couldn't reasonably expect to get to Hawaii someday, so you add it to the list. The obstacle may be financing the trip, and this falls into the Opportunity step of the Approach, so we'll talk about it again there. For now, as long as you could physically travel to Hawaii (e.g. you could travel in a plane for several hours), put it on the list.

However, if one of your goals is to have a good relationship with a relative with whom there has been a history of conflict or abuse, this could be much more difficult to achieve. It would necessitate either you or the other person, or both, making personality or character changes in order to have a lasting positive relationship, in addition to the time required to rebuild trust in the relationship.

As you can see, identifying goals can be quite easy, but accomplishing them could be quite a different story. For now, just list the goals. Don't intellectualize them or consider whether or not you will be able to accomplish them.

One of the most common choices people struggle with is a career choice or change. Many students do not spend time thinking about the things in which they excel or what their passions are, when thinking about the choice of a career. Noted exceptions are those wonderfully talented musicians, actors, and other professionals who have always had a prominent gift that propelled them to a specific career path.

Many young adults go into college without a clear picture of what they want to explore. Many who have chosen a path are unaware of how little they know about the realities of living that chosen path, thus eventually becoming disillusioned or unhappy.

By making choices based on your passion, or the things in which you excel, you move significantly farther toward the chance to have a rewarding and fulfilling life.

Start by asking yourself, "What do I love to do?"

If the answers include things you are currently doing, great! But you are reading this book for a reason, probably because you do want to make changes in your life. Keep working on your list until you have several items on it that you love, whether or not they currently exist in your life.

If the answers to the question "What do I love to do?" do not include your current lifestyle components, you'll know that the changes you eventually choose will be positive changes because they will be based on having more of the things you love in your life.

The answers to "What do I love to do?" may not come easily to you. If this is the case, consider some personality typing resources. Stay away from the monthly magazine quizzes, but invest in one or two good books about personality types and career matching.

There are many excellent books on the market that will help you explore your personality type. Knowing your personality type could be put to use in your life work. I've listed some of them in the resource guide in the back of this book.

You could also spend some time with an insightful good friend or life partner, a therapist or life coach, who will help you sort out your strengths and desires, further clarifying your choices. If you choose one of these options, please make sure it is someone who truly has your best interest at heart, and who knows how to be supportive through the exploration process.

After identifying what it is you love to do, the next step in identifying change choices and goals is to think about the things in which you excel. In order to make changes, especially if the change desired is a career change, you need to determine your capabilities. What else can you do besides what you are doing today?

Remember the list you made when you were reading the first chapters of this book? This was the list of all the things at which you excel. Get out that list, and review it. Add whatever comes to mind that didn't make it onto the list in the first round. Keep working on it until you've added five to ten examples of ways in which you excel. Remember, it's okay to boast a little—it's your own list.

Once you have your "What do I love to do?" and "Things at which I excel" lists, take the time to sit quietly, perhaps ask the higher power in which you believe for help, and see if there are things you could add. Write down any impressions or thoughts you have, even if your conscious mind is being negative about them. Do not judge them at this stage. Open up, get out of your comfort zone, and out of the box you perceive yourself to be in based on the things society has taught you. Let the thoughts and impressions and dreams all come out. Write them down as they come to you.

For instance, if you've always been an office professional, but you have a good voice, put singer on the list. It will be difficult, but don't judge your list items right now—just put down things you do well and positive characteristics you have. Push the "yes, but…" conflicts of the conscious mind away for a little while.

Just write—try not to evaluate or judge whether or not you could actually make a living at what you are writing down. All you want to do at this point is create a list of passions, positive traits, and talents. Don't worry about whether they seem feasible.

> *"If you limit your choices only to what seems possible or reasonable, you disconnect yourself from what you truly want, and all that is left is a compromise."*
>
> **Robert Fritz**
> Author, *Your Life As Art*

After this exercise you will have a list of the things you could consider as choices for change, and ultimately as choices for your goals. Continue to add to this list as you think of things in the days to come. You'll find as you pay attention to this, more things will be apparent to you as your mind opens to considering things you would not previously have considered.

Choice #4: *Choose to be aware.*

Pay attention to what's going on around you. Frequently, we get messages by being aware of what's taking place around us. We see someone doing something and think, "I could do that." Add it to the list. Think outside the box on this one. In my seminars, people often work until they come up with three full pages of things they could do, no matter how silly or unrealistic some of them seem at the time.

By now you should have a list of at least three values that resonate with you, as well as a list of things you love and things at which you excel. These will predictably be closely aligned to your answer to the question, "What are my passions?"

Don't do anything else with the list for two weeks, except to add to it based on what you see and hear and feel around you, or to make notes about which things on the list have been affirmed by things you see and hear and feel. Be aware of how frequently you will be reminded of the items on the list as you go through your daily routine. Notice which items on your list are being affirmed by actions and reactions around you.

Being aware will also come into play when we talk about opportunity in the next chapter. For now, just watch and listen.

Make a conscious choice to abide with your new list and your options for a little while.

The next step will be to prioritize the list; then you will formulate a plan for how to make the changes you choose and how to succeed in reaching the goals you choose. In some cases, it may be relatively simple. Others may require more effort. You may need to go back to school for training. You may need to obtain a license to practice what you've chosen. You may need to resign from an existing role in order to pursue this new dream. There's one thing you have to do, even if the answer is simple and already apparent to you.

Wait!

Don't do anything yet. Just live with your list for a while. The next elements of the plan have to be considered fully before any steps are taken. You may choose to talk with your spouse, partner, or good friend, but don't move forward with any of the plans yet. Let the choices sink in. Meditate about your list; listen to what messages you may receive from your inner self, from the outer world, and from your own higher authority.

These choices are based on your values and your passions. Consider how these choices make you feel physically as you think about each one. If the feelings you get when you think about it are excitement and joy, and your body is rested and peaceful, you are on the right track. If you are feeling tense, your shoulders or neck ache, or your stomach is in knots, then the choice or goal you are thinking about may not be one that ends up high on your priority list.

> ## Choice #5: *Choose your priorities.*

Once you've lived with your list for a while, it will become clear to you which things you feel strongly about, and which are just passing fancies or pipe dreams.

Begin to prioritize your list, based on which things mean the most to you. In other words, which things are you most passionate about, or which things will you seriously regret if you never accomplish them?

When considering your priorities, review your notes from the waiting period. If you had negative physical sensations, thoughts, or anxiety about a particular item, put a minus sign next to it. If you had joyful, peaceful feelings or thoughts, or felt extreme excitement when contemplating a particular item, put a check mark next to that item.

Now, without giving it too much thought, do a quick numerical prioritization of this list. Your highest priority (the accomplishment, goal, or choice you want to succeed at the most) will be number 1, the second number 2, and so on, until you have assigned a value to everything on the list.

If there is anything in the top ten items that also has a minus sign next to it, you may have to go back to the first steps to consider whether this is really a good choice for you to make, or a good goal to set.

Choice #6: *Choose to be patient.*

When you set priorities for your choices and goals, and find that some of your top choices also are those that make you feel most anxious, it is important to look at what fears are causing these physical symptoms when you think about this choice in your life. If you are feeling anxious with a choice, sit quietly, or meditate about the change being considered and the physical symptoms those considerations are causing.

Let your mind wander through the possibilities of "What If" land. You might want to use a page in your notebook to set up the page like the sample shown. Write in all the things you think could go wrong in the "What If?" column. Then put the worst case scenarios in the "Then What?" column. When you write these things down, it is often easier to see the improbability of many of our fears. Most of these "what if's" will never happen, but we cling to them anyway. We need to let go of the fear, and embrace the challenges of positive change.

What If?	Then What?

Take some time with this. It's not an overnight process. One of the most effective ways to bring about positive change is to find an accountability partner. Gee, another choice! This can be a spouse, relative, or close friend. The person you select must be someone you trust and who trusts you completely, who will be honest with you, not hurtful or vengeful or jealous, and will be caring and understanding. Rather than a relative, many people choose a friend or life coach because there is less emotional baggage from the relationship to get in the way of progress.

Make an arrangement to talk regularly, whether it's daily, every other day, or once a week. We all need to share our goals (and our "what if" fears) with someone who will gently help us on our journey, someone who will celebrate our achievements no matter how small, and will remind us of our goals when we fall short. It's almost impossible to make real change totally on our own.

Be patient. You could be dealing with a choice that involves one of the biggest decisions of your life. Or you could be working on a choice that has to do with something less life altering. Regardless of the seriousness of your choice, take time with it, to think, feel, and act it through.

If waiting is new to you because you are used to acting on your choices immediately, think about how making the choice to wait affects you—again, feel this physically and mentally. Make notes in your notebook about these thoughts and feelings. They may be telling you something about the choice itself, or how you deal with a specific type of situation. It is usually a significant learning experience.

If you've purchased this book with an existing knowledge of the things you want to change in your life, and need the how-to instructions, I encourage you meditate on the changes and goals you've set as well. Abide with them. Wait. Continue to read on, and see if you gain more insight about your choice or decision as a result.

Choice #7: *Choose to persevere.*

Focus. Focus. Focus. Stick to the target. Keep your goal in sight. Don't give up. Never give up.

When you have completed the tasks of identifying and prioritizing your goals, you will move into the next step of creating and being aware of opportunities. With every step of The CORE Approach™ there are choices. It is a pervasive concept affecting all the others.

As you move into the Opportunities step there may be times when giving up and conceding that something was a bad choice seems prudent. Before you throw in the towel, make sure that you are not doing it for the wrong reasons. There may be legitimate reasons to give up. More likely is the reality that a decision is made to "cut the losses" because success is more difficult than had been anticipated, the sacrifice now seems too great, or the opportunities do not appear sufficiently abundant.

"The person who makes a success of living is the one who sees his goal steadily and aims for it unswervingly. That is dedication."
Cecil B. DeMille (1881-1959)

Many new businesses fail because the founders do not allow ample time for success to happen, often because of improper or insufficient planning, and frequently because of errors in execution of whatever plan is in place.

The same is true of individuals with new goals. Allow yourself a reasonable time in which to achieve your goals. If it seems as if you are failing, and it is a goal about which you are passionate, determine to persevere.

If you find yourself ready to give up, think about whether or not this is a pattern in your life. Each new generation gets increasingly spoiled by new technology, inventions and ideas that make it easier to succeed. When success isn't achieved right away, there is a tendency to move on to the next thing, rather than, as my father would have said, "Put some elbow grease into it!"

If things aren't going well, identify what and where the plan to achieve is failing, and work through what needs to change in order to achieve success. Perseverance is the key to ensuring that the identification of passion, attainment of knowledge, and overcoming fears to get to the point of courageousness has not been in vain.

See it through. Focus on the result.

Choice #8: *Choose to be intentional.*

The simple act of making a choice implies intention. Make each act, based on each choice made, and every goal identified, intentional. What I mean by this is that every movement or action toward accomplishment of your goals should have an identified risk probability and a specific expected result.

If you thought about your values as you read Choice #2, you may have already made a choice about a certain value that you feel is at the core or base of your life. Be intentional about reinforcing that value in your everyday actions. Think about your choices and goals and the priorities determined by your values as you go through each day.

Make a weekly to-do list that is based on moving farther toward your goals. Intentionality is a big factor in the other steps of The CORE Approach™ as well, since every decision you make in each step is geared toward achievement of success.

Using The CORE Approach™ is a life change, not a passing fad. Be intentional about learning each step, thinking about consciously using the steps in your life, integrating the concepts into your personality, and then passing it along to others as part of your responsibility.

> **You can accomplish the goals
> you set for yourself.**

It may not always be easy or without sacrifice, but with proper planning, skill, courage and perseverance, any goal is within reach.

*"Opportunity is missed by most people because
it is dressed in overalls and looks like work."*
Thomas A. Edison (1847-1931)

Chapter 8   Opportunity

Opportunity knocks. Or does it?

Just as many of us wait for life to happen to us, many of us also wait for opportunities to come our way. The premise of The CORE Approach™ is that you live your life fully and experience everything that you possibly can. With this in mind, it stands to reason that if you wait for opportunities, you might not want the opportunities that come your way, or you may never get the opportunities you want and need to obtain your goals. So, what's the answer to this dilemma?

Go get them! Opportunities are all around you—seek them out! Find opportunities that will move you closer to your goals, to the choices you've made. Steven Covey, in his best-selling book *The Seven Habits of Highly Effective People*, lists "Be Proactive" as the first of the seven habits.

Being proactive and being intentional go hand in hand. Seek opportunities everywhere you go. Use your passion about your goals to show your spirit to the people you meet. Talk to people about their experiences and yours, about your desires and goals. Chances are that by talking to others about what you are working toward, you will uncover opportunities through those people. Be willing and open to see these opportunities when they present themselves. Sometimes we are not aware that we are staring in the face of an opportunity because it was not presented to us in the manner we would have expected. View every encounter as an opportunity that your higher power has given you to move a step further toward achieving success.

Opportunities are always around you.

Think about who might be in your circle of influence that can help you achieve your goals and create opportunities for you. Look at your family and friends in this new light. Can any of them provide opportunities for you, either directly, or by introducing you to someone in their network? Consider colleagues, former co-workers, former clients, college professors, your religious leaders, or people you know through clubs and organizations, even if the club or organization is not related to what you are currently working toward.

Look beyond your immediate family and circle of friends. Move into your ex-mediate circle. (Yes, I know ex-mediate isn't a Webster or Oxford Dictionary word—it's a real word, though—I know because I made it up. It's the opposite of immediate.) What this means is that you work through your immediate circle of influence into the outer circle, or the ex-mediate circle of influence and contact and talk with those people, via introductions from your immediate circle.

Network, network, and then network some more. Ask people how you can help them, whether they have time to provide feedback on your idea, or what a good networking contact would be for them. If you are willing to extend yourself (intentionally!), you will generally find that the other person will be more than happy to reciprocate. It is constantly amazing to me how many doors are opened by simply asking others how you can help them, or what they need from you.

For years, I worked on charity events in fund-raising roles. I had several friends who would wryly comment, "You'll ask anyone for anything." This was especially common when I'd interrupt our lunch conversation to ask the restaurant owner for a gift certificate donation for the charity auction or a door prize. My reply to my friend was always the same. "Yes, you are right. If you don't ask, you can't get what you want or need. And the worst thing that will happen is that the other person will say no. Then I will thank them for their time and move on."

Mark Victor Hansen, in one of his earlier sets of educational audiotapes, talks about using a technique called the "A-S-K to G-E-T" method of identifying opportunities. This resonates with my "I have nothing to lose by asking" mentality, and has stayed with me over the years. I quote him regularly in my seminars and articles, always giving him the credit, of course.

Think about it. What's the worst that can happen? If you have been polite and respectful in your request, the worst that will happen (the "what-if") will be that the other person will decline your request. So, you will thank them for taking the time to talk with you, and move on. Then ask, "What's next?" and proceed to create your next opportunity.

What other methods can you use to create opportunities? Think about who you don't know that you need to know. There are people right in your own community you can access. Try your local Chamber of Commerce. See who is in their directory that might provide an opportunity or two, or might further your movement toward your goal. Go to local networking events and seminars and get to know people in the community. Contact people you meet at these events and ask for a meeting. Many of them will be more than happy to accommodate your request. You'll be surprised how many opportunities come from simply developing relationships.

> **It is your responsibility to find or create opportunities for the life you want.**

What about already successful people in your field of interest? Determine how you can meet those people, by going to their presentations and talks, buying tickets to their shows, contacting them through their web sites, writing letters, or other creative means. Be careful here—you don't want to be accused of being a stalker. Make sure that your contact method is professional and that the correspondence has meaning to it. You might want to talk with someone in marketing for the best approach before you decide to contact an executive or celebrity.

The bottom line is that there are many opportunities out there for those who seek them. One method I employ is that I sit quietly and ask my Higher Authority for guidance for the specific goal I am working toward accomplishing. Then listen for the guidance. Now, understand that this is not always an immediate answer, and I'm not a lunatic who hears voices. However, my belief is that if you listen, the universe or God or whatever higher authority exists in your belief system, will provide you with answers. These may be words you "hear," it may be a conversation you have soon after your request for guidance, or it may be an actual opportunity that seems to drop into your lap unsolicited.

Pay attention. Remember those words from earlier? One aspect of identifying opportunities is awareness, and paying attention. It has been my experience that once an idea is out there, you begin to get responses. The responses aren't always answers, but more often than not, they will provide some sort of affirmation that you are on the right path, if indeed, you are.

Where will I find an opportunity today?

Again, look for the non-obvious, and don't make assumptions. Just because someone you know from a photography class at school doesn't seem interested in anything but photography, ask how you can help that person toward his or her goals. That conversation should lead to what you need as well, and you get to talk about your goals. That soon-to-be photographer just might know your primary investor, and provide the introduction you need to get the funding for your product or business!

Pay attention! I can't emphasize this enough. View every interaction you have in the outside world as a potential opportunity. There are no coincidences in life. We all have to be aware of the opportunities that present themselves. So often, we don't realize that something has the potential to come our way, because we are too busy being judgmental.

How do you limit yourself with your preconceived ideas?

Think how often you've brushed off a stranger who tried to strike up a conversation in a line in which you were waiting, or you avoided talking to someone who looked or dressed differently than yourself. These may have been people who could have had just the answer to a problem with which you'd been struggling, or perhaps provided you with a name of someone who could help you with your goal.

Opportunities may not arrive in the way, shape, or form that you expect.

I've had experiences that have taught me time and again to be open to whatever possibility may surface, not to try to control or steer an opportunity a certain way. The cover of this book is a prime example. The artist who designed the cover is a good friend and colleague. We talked numerous times about the concepts in the book and the resultant seminars and educational materials. A cross-sectioned apple, with seeds showing at the core, is prominent in all the educational material artwork.

In my infinite wisdom, I evidently let it be known that I had an expectation that the apple and tree should be on the book cover as well. My friend, the artist, being the caring and supportive soul that she is, designed a cover for me that she thought I wanted. The result was one that neither of us really cared for.

When she told me she had another idea, but hadn't presented it when I seemed intent on the tree concept, I told her to run with it. The result was spectacular, as you now know, since the cover probably had something to do with attracting you to this book!

Just remember, we aren't here to judge or to control, but we are here to live the best life we possibly can. That means achieving all we possibly can, and making the choices and seeking the opportunities to move toward goals we set for ourselves.

It also means keeping an open mind. Answers come in unexpected packages, and when we are quick to judge and make assumptions for others, we miss these answers and opportunities.

My husband and I recently saw the movie *Bruce Almighty*. Although a comedy, there are some very real lessons in that movie. There's a scene where Jim Carrey, as Bruce, is driving down a street, furious about his life, screaming at God to show him a sign. He's following a truck full of street signs that say "Wrong Way" and "Do Not Enter" and the like. Ignoring this, he speeds around the truck and ends up in an auto accident. Like the movie, we often fail to heed the very signs we ask for, because they seem too mundane or obvious. Look around.

In opportunity seeking, as a means to succeeding—you have not only to open your mind, but truly to open your heart to this huge universe of opportunity, to those opportunities that move you ever closer, one step at a time, toward your purpose.

What are some of the things you can do to increase opportunities? Certainly, you can advertise if you are looking for business opportunities. Marketing and advertising, based on strategic planning, will work to identify opportunities for you.

Join organizations, clubs, and associations related to your area of interest. When I say join, that includes participate in the events sponsored by the club or organization. Simply writing a check for membership dues is not going to do much to create opportunities. Applying for and receiving approval for membership will get you listed in the organization's directory. That's about it. And there is some value to that, since club members will generally seek out other club members first when they need something.

Think how much more opportunity will be created by going to events and talking with people about your synergies, where you might work together or help one another.

Volunteering is another opportunity that most people don't recognize. When you volunteer, even though you may not be directly furthering your goals, or even feel as though you are taking time and focus away from your goals, you get an opportunity to develop relationships. Through these relationships, and by getting to know you, the contacts you make will remember you and discuss you with others, or refer others to you when they know there is a similar interest or potential for you and their contact to help one another.

Create some sort of "leave-behind" item. Whether it's a traditional business card, a brochure about your goal, or a gimmicky item, like an imprinted pen, notepad, or coffee cup, pick something to leave behind. When you leave something behind, the person with whom you left the item will think of you again.

Look around. Think about your choices. Open your mind and your heart to your purpose. Judge not. Talk up your goals. Be aware of your surroundings. Think about the people you meet and speak with in light of your goals and purpose. Seek out those opportunities, or those opportunity providers or facilitators.

"We make a living by what we get, we make a life by what we give."

Sir Winston Churchill (1874-1965)

Chapter 9   Responsibility

We all have responsibilities. Some of us take them more seriously than others, but we all have them. Responsibility, as it relates to the CORE concepts, has to do with being responsible about what we achieve and what we do with the abundance we begin to see through use of this approach. When we make solid, educated choices about our goals, and create opportunities to make things happen, we WILL begin to have more abundance in our lives. Responsibility has to do with how you handle that abundance.

Giving is our right and our responsibility.

We all have the responsibility to give. As children and adolescents, we go through a learning process whereby in the first stage of learning, the ego, or self, is of primary concern. As we begin to be aware of others, through parental teaching, intuition, and watching the modeling of others, we begin to learn compassion. At least, I hope we all learn compassion!

In the earlier stages, before adulthood, the intention to give may or may not be present, depending on our upbringing and insight.

Entering into adulthood, when we begin to realize that we truly have gifts and experiences and knowledge, there is more opportunity and possibility that we will begin to share these things with others. I believe that there is an immutable law of the universe that compels us to give of our abundance, in whatever form that may be. Failure to give results in a stunting of our abundance, or at least in a failure of it to thrive or grow. The more we give, especially when the giving is without the expectation of receiving in return, the more we ultimately gain.

> ## We receive exponentially more than we give.

Now, I've been talking about giving of our abundance. What does that mean? As we know, abundance means having more than enough. "More than enough of what?" you might ask. I would answer that with another question—what is it that you feel you can give to others? That is the substance or gift of which you have abundance.

People think they have to give money, and worry that there won't be enough money left to live on or raise their family. We don't always need to give money. What else do you have to give?

We can give time, advice, ideas, tangible items, stories and legends, music, and a multitude of other things. Giving does not have to be monetary. We can give of ourselves, in the form of mentoring, being a big brother or sister, coaching, idea tithing, volunteering, fund raising, or any other number of ways we could think of pertaining to our lives and where we want to be giving.

Tangible giving could mean cleaning out a closet for a clothing drive, giving outgrown children's clothing to a less fortunate family with small children, cooking for a local soup kitchen, or donating a car or household items that are no longer needed.

How can I help?

When I do consulting with business groups, and use The CORE Approach™, I always recommend that their teambuilding include doing something together that is non-work related. I've had teams elect to go to Habitat for Humanity together for a day or a week and build houses. Or they work a Special Olympics day as volunteers, or take a regular rotation cooking and serving in a local food shelter. There are a variety of things from which to choose when determining an avenue of giving.

As a business owner, for instance, one might decide to hire physically or developmentally disabled individuals. This will open jobs for these people, and help them not only to earn a living, but also to increase their feeling of self-worth and self-esteem, because it allows them to give as well. Many people who are not as readily employable, for whatever reason—it doesn't have to be a disability—find that they begin to discover their own purpose when someone gives them a chance to show what they can do.

As a working adult, perhaps a way of giving back could be coaching. There are many community leagues and teams that need more coaches, whether or not you have a child on the team. And you may just discover, or rediscover, passion for a sport you had long forgotten—especially when a child comes to you, gives you a high-five, and says, "Thanks, Coach!"

Where can I help?

You have choices about how and where you can help. In addition to those mentioned above, you can be a Big Brother or Big Sister, join a Reading Is Fun program, volunteer at the Boys and Girls Clubs, help out at your church, synagogue, or place of worship, spend a day or more working for Habitat for Humanity—just to name a few ways and places you can help others.

Of course, let us not leave money out completely. There are many of us who do follow scripture which calls for traditional religious tithing. In scripture, this is a gift to the religious sect of a percentage of all that one has in their possession. There is nothing wrong with giving money, if that is your abundance. I've never seen any charitable cause turn down cash. Think about it...what would you do with that $10 anyway? Stop at Wendy's on the way home? Give it away instead, and then go home and make a peanut butter and jelly sandwich.

Whatever you choose to give, do it joyfully, and without regret or selfishness. Only giving in this spirit will truly fulfill the soul and enable your spirit to be free to recognize and seek the opportunities that will come your way as a result.

> *"You must give some time to your fellow men. Even if it's a little thing, do something for others - something for which you get no pay but the privilege of doing it."*
> **Albert Schweitzer (1875-1965)**

So, what does this have to do with The CORE Approach™? When you begin to realize how different your life can be by making conscious choices and finding the opportunities, you will find yourself telling people what is happening in your life. This is the beginning of the giving. You are giving hope to others who want to make changes, but are fearful.

By writing this book, it is my prayer and earnest wish that these words and this concept will provide you with hope that you, too, can determine what is not abundant in your life, and make the change to have that abundance.

You need to be a witness to others as well, as you begin to utilize these concepts and see changes starting to happen. Provide the hope that they, too, can make the positive changes they so desperately desire in their lives. Giving isn't always about dollars and cents. But as you begin to better your financial circumstances through these strategies, you need to make sure that you are giving in some way as well as receiving.

Giving is also about idea sharing, giving hope and encouragement, and sharing your confidence that positive change is possible. Many people don't believe that it is possible for them. I can tell you, without a doubt, that it is possible for every person who truly desires change and takes the steps to make those changes. But that last phrase is the key. YOU have to take the steps to make the changes. YOU have to STOP letting life just happen. As my friend Scott Schilling preaches, "Success is Your Responsibility!"

Give to others. No matter what you believe, I'm here to tell you that the more you help others, the more abundance finds you.

Have you ever been really down and feeling terrible, when someone who also felt really down called you to talk, and you listened to their troubles? As you listened, and you tried to help them, didn't you forget about your own issues and actually begin to feel better because of the help you were providing? If you haven't ever had this experience, try it. Next time you feel down, see who's around that you can help with something. As you help them, your difficulties seem to lessen and you feel better.

This is increasingly true when you are not thinking about what you are going to get back. The most rewarding situations of giving for me have been when I've been able to do something totally anonymously for someone else. It is not about the recognition—it is about knowing that you were able to help, and that you took the steps to help when others did not. There's a self-satisfaction in giving in this way that surpasses the satisfaction that would come from any third-party recognition.

Helping is helping. No matter what method you employ, if you are giving to and helping others, it will come back to you exponentially.

You may not even realize that you are giving to someone else. Perhaps you will talk with someone about how excited you are that positive changes are happening for you, as a result of your choices and opportunity awareness. You may never know in the future, but that particular conversation could be the spark that enables the other person to begin to think about their own capability for positive change.

As you make changes in your life, you have a responsibility to be a positive example to others. I'm not asking you to be an evangelist. I am asking you to share yourself—whether it takes the form of your ideas, your time, your money, or your services. As you do, you will be pleasantly surprised by how much you continue to receive.

> *"Real integrity is doing the right thing, knowing that nobody's going to know whether you did it or not."*
>
> **Oprah Winfrey (1954-)**

"Many of life's failures are people who did not realize how close they were to success when they gave up."

Thomas A. Edison (1847-1931)

Chapter 10   Expectation

Expectation is anticipating, or looking forward. Both Oxford and Webster dictionaries include "looking forward" in their definitions of the word expectation.

Take a little time to think about the following question:

What are your expectations?

If I were to guess, I'd say that your answers to that question have to do with other people and events. You might have some of the following as your answers:

- I expect others to treat me fairly.
- I expect my children to listen to me when I tell them something.
- I expect to be paid for the work I do.
- I expect summer to come after spring and before autumn.
- I expect the sun to come up tomorrow.

I'd like to ask you to take a different view of expectations for the first part of the discussion in this chapter. I want to view this chapter first from the perspective of your expectations of yourself.

Let's change the question, just slightly.

> ## What are your expectations of yourself?

Was this question more or less difficult to answer than the first version of the question? My guess is that it was more difficult.

If you are using a notebook as you go through this book, take a moment and write your answers to this question in the notebook. If you have been unable to come up with any answers to this question, keep the notebook handy, and as you continue to read, write down the self-expectations that come to mind. Don't worry about whether they are positive or negative at this point. Just make a note of them.

What are some of the possible answers you could have? Here are some that have arisen in my seminars:

- I expect my life to be difficult.
- I expect freedom.
- I expect to work for everything I get or have.
- I expect to be working all my life.
- I expect to have children.
- I expect to get a new car next year.
- I expect not much.

Were any of these answers your answers? The answers above are real answers people have given me to this question in recent months. Did you notice that some of these answers have a sense of very little expectation of excitement or joy?

This is typical. Very few people, when asked this question will answer:

- I expect my life to be filled with peace, joy, and abundance.
- I expect to be a multi-millionaire.
- I expect to be successful at the things I undertake with careful and considered choice, opportunity, and responsibility.

How surprised would you be if someone answered you in this way? Why is it that most people would be surprised if they heard someone utter these statements? A typical response might be a sarcastic "Yeah, right!"

We're all great at believing the negative things people tell us, and the things we consequently learn about ourselves. Things like "I'm not smart enough to do this," or "I need to lose weight so that people will like me more." It's much harder for us to believe positive things about ourselves. This is evidenced in many of the personal statements we tell ourselves, consciously or subconsciously, every day. We all have doubts, and these doubts about ourselves surface readily at the first sign of difficulty or trouble in our lives.

They're shown by the mother whose child is not doing as well as expected in school, and she wonders what she's done wrong. Or by the manager who meets with an employee who has decided to take another position, and he thinks that perhaps he didn't meet the employee's needs. Or by responding to our spouse, who may be in a more quiet mood than usual, and wondering if it's been caused by something we've done or said.

We tend to be very good a beating up on ourselves and minimizing our expectations. We tend to believe that we cannot achieve, rather than expect success of ourselves. We tend to believe that we are not good enough, smart enough, attractive enough, rich enough, thin enough, or funny enough. We see ourselves as mediocre at best, and among the bulk of the population, not standing out at all.

In contrast, it's much more difficult to conjure up the positive images of ourselves. Expectation, the fourth element in The CORE Approach™, is about having and holding the highest possible expectation of ourselves. If you can make choices about the changes you want to make, and seek the opportunities to make those changes happen, while enabling your sense of responsibility, how can you fail? Your internal expectation has to be set on success.

So, the first expectation you need to set, especially in times of changes in your life, is your own. What do you know, without a doubt, and even in difficult times, is true about you?

We have to stop being so hard on ourselves. I use the "Things at which I excel" exercise in seminars and training classes to help people begin to learn to be nicer to themselves. Remember that exercise from earlier in the book? Take out that list and review it again now. Can you add anything to it? Take the time to add anything new you have thought about as you've been reading. Review this list regularly, and add to it when you can. There is nothing wrong with believing in yourself.

We've been taught not to boast or talk up our accomplishments, and I agree that in excess, or in constant conversations with others, this can be tiresome and perhaps obnoxious behavior. However, when it comes to our internal messages, we cannot take enough time to overcome all of the negativity society has heaped on us throughout our years on this earth.

Be good to yourself. Remind yourself of your positive traits and accomplishments. This is the place from which comes the positive self-expectation. Expect success. Expect accomplishment as you choose your life changes. Expect that you will have the life you want to have.

Here are some ideas for continuing to explore your self-expectation changes. Think of positive affirmations about yourself, preferably in regard to the situation you find yourself in, or the changes you want. An affirmation is a positive statement, such as: "I know that I am an educated and experienced business person, and can tackle difficult situations such as _____ at work." It can be a simple "I like the person I am, and so will others," statement.

Perhaps your change goal is to lose 20 pounds. One of the things you've identified yourself as being good at is learning new things. Use that concept, in a different sense, to enable yourself to succeed.

For example, "I am good at learning new things, so that means I can learn to make consistently better food choices in order to lose 20 pounds and be healthier."

Other affirmations might be things such as:

- When I make conscious choices by listening to my inner voice and following my passions, I am successful.

- I am an excellent researcher, so I can find all the information I need to make choices and decisions about the career possibilities to follow my passion for _____.

- I have a great voice and a passion for music, so I can be successful in the field of music by researching the opportunities and being creative about looking beyond traditional choices and finding or creating something that uses my talents.

Repeat these affirmations often to yourself. (Some therapists may even tell you to do this in front of the mirror.) Write them down, and keep them somewhere you can review them often.

Setting your internal expectations sounds like it is an easy thing to do. For most of us, it is not very easy to do, although it is not a difficult concept to understand. Integration of this concept into our psyche, our very being, is a much more difficult task. This is not an overnight, one-shot accomplishment. The more difficult these exercises were for you, the longer it will take to begin to think instinctively in positive terms of success.

Constant reminders will help. As recommended earlier, keep your journal or notebook nearby, and review the lists and affirmations at least weekly. Enlist a spouse or good friend to remind you of the affirmations. It might feel awkward at first, but you'll be surprised at how willing someone who cares about you will be to tell you something good about yourself. They may not do it without being asked, or without being given the script, but my bet is that they will be more than happy to oblige when the positive change in you becomes apparent.

Believing in you leads to feeling better about yourself. It's a natural extension of the affirmation. When we get positive attention, our self-esteem rises and we react more positively to ourselves and to others, especially to the person providing the affirmation to us. I'm not prone to providing marital advice, but asking a spouse to provide an affirmation to you could just be the key to a happier marriage!

Imagine how you would feel if your spouse regularly and sincerely provided the affirmation, "Honey, you are intelligent and creative and I know that you will succeed in finding the right career choice." Chances are you will feel good about yourself (after all, you are intelligent and creative) and you will believe that the right career is just around the corner (remember, you will be successful in finding the right career choice).

Your reaction to your spouse will probably be a thank you in words, a hug, or other gesture of appreciation. This, in turn, enables your spouse to feel cared about and appreciated. See where this is going? Try it. You might be amazed at the results.

As you begin to achieve your goal and see that the process works, this reinforces the affirmations and helps you continue to use the process. As it becomes more natural to you, you will find yourself setting more positive self-expectations. Eventually, this will become a new habit that becomes part of the positive change in you, and you will be able to pass it on to others as you have learned it.

The expectation of success is one type of self-expectation. There are others. Your reactions are also a type of self-expectation. Think about the way you react to situations. Are your reactions predictable?

How do you expect yourself to react when someone pulls out in front of you on the road? What about when someone spills something on the just-mopped floor?

Are you calm, or do you react with indignation, anger, or other negative reaction? At times, we may think that our anger reaction is justified, but in reality, these types of stress reactions use more energy and are more damaging than we realize.

Reactions are self expectations. You have the power to change your reactions.

**Change the way you expect
yourself to react.**

Even when we think we are justified in yelling at someone, or in reacting with an angry tone or action, there is a tendency to second guess our reaction once the situation that caused the reaction has passed.

How often has a stressed-out mother reacted with a harsh admonition to a child who has just spilled his milk? Although the parent is angry that she now has to clean up the mess and may feel that the anger is justified, as the situation clears, more often than not she will feel bad that she yelled at the child for an accidental mishap, perhaps even to the point of apologizing. For many mothers, this is not even the end of the event. Many mothers will then stay awake at bedtime ruminating on what a terrible mother she must be for chastising a small child for an accident.

The energy wasted on guilt would be much better used in resetting her expectation to react more calmly and kindly.

Think of the manager who puts an employee down for not following a directive to the letter. Perhaps the manager was not explicit in his or her instructions, and had given an expectation that the employee could not understand. Perhaps the deadline was tight. Whatever the reason, if the manager was stressed at the time the assignment came to deadline, the reaction of belittling the worker would, to some, seem justified. This same manager, under a less stressed demeanor, might have sat down with the employee and discussed what he or she did not understand in the original directions that resulted in the poor outcome.

**Your reactions are your choice
and your responsibility.**

Almost all of us have a different reaction mode to situations when we are happy and not stressed than we have when we are under stress. Expectations play a role here as well.

Set your own expectation for how you will react in times of stress. We tend to regress toward our comfort zone in difficult times, even when that comfort zone is not good for us. Think ahead and do some introspective role playing, in order to see yourself handling your self-thoughts positively in times of stress, so that you will be prepared when the stress hits.

If your style has always been to get upset and begin to raise your voice when the stress begins, begin to envision a calmer you, with an even voice tone, handling the situation in a confident manner. Think through scenarios which could bring out your negative style, and change the scene to reflect the positive approach you want to use. It's a bit like a mental rehearsal. If you use this method, you will find that as time passes, the more positive approach is the one you use, because it has become familiar to you through rehearsal. Consequently, you begin to get more and more comfortable with it. You have effectively changed your comfort zone to this new behavior, and will come to expect it of yourself.

Change your behavior by changing your expectations.

There are assessments you can take that will identify traits and characteristics both at times of comfort and times of stress. A good therapist can help you with these assessments. However, being truthfully introspective will yield similar results, if you can do it. Sometimes the most difficult person to be truthful with is you.

Here's an exercise to try. Being brutally honest with yourself, think about recent situations in which you have reacted negatively to something. Jot these down in your notebook. If the situation is no longer emotionally charged, think about how you could have handled the situation differently, and more positively. By reviewing these actions after they occur, and envisioning yourself reacting in a more positive manner, you will begin to condition yourself to behave this way when a difficult situation occurs.

Again, this is a change in behavior which needs to become a habit and a self-expectation. When you begin behaving in a more positive manner in difficult situations, you realize you have learned to master the art of handling emotionally charged occurrences. One result is that positive self-worth and self-esteem increases. This sets off yet another self-expectation of success.

Now we come to the idea of expectations that you cannot control — those of other people. Although you cannot control how others will feel, react, or behave, you can set their expectations by your own actions, reactions, words, and behavior.

This is the external expectation you need to set — the one for others around you. How you see yourself, and how the world sees you, will determine how the world treats you. Your self-expectations, your personal affirmations, and your faith in yourself (along with whatever spiritual power receives your faith) will guide others to the treatment you deserve. In other words, when you are confident and treating yourself well, others will have confidence in you and treat you with respect.

Once you have mastered the art of positive self-expectation, or at least once you have understood and validated the process, you will begin to think again about others' expectations. You can set these expectations, rather than accepting whatever comes your way from others.

> ## Set the expectation for the behavior you want to see in others.

One of the big hurdles I faced when I began thinking about changing my career, was getting my family on board with the new ideas and the resultant new schedule and working arrangements. My husband was worried about the dollars, especially the paycheck that would no longer be coming in every other week with my name on it. The children needed to learn that I was working, even though I was at home, and that they could not come in and spend time in my office on their computer every afternoon.

This meant I had to educate my husband on what it was I wanted to do, how I planned to accomplish those things, and keep him informed about progress to ease his stress level. He has become sufficiently comfortable (especially after the first big client came in) that he has recently even relinquished some of his bookcase space in the office, moving his things into another area of the house.

Another outside expectation that needed to be set was that of the friends who live nearby and would call to go to lunch, or want to spend the afternoon shopping. I have a number of friends who are hard-working, stay-at-home moms. They have flexibility when their children are in school, like I do, but the difference is that their work will often include going to the stores in the area, running errands, and other household related tasks. There were people who thought I was being snobbish by not joining them on their rounds, and I had to help them understand that I really was working and running a business, even if it was happening from my home, and not from an office elsewhere.

I did make allowances for the children (who, at this time were teenagers) to use their computer (which is in my office across from my desk and my computer) if they were doing research, or even writing a paper, as long as I wasn't writing. When I write, I really need to concentrate on what I'm doing, and being interrupted with questions about formatting a paper or how to spell something that they are researching is very distracting.

I don't want any of you parents out there to be upset with me, thinking that I was keeping the kids from being able to do their school work. I adjusted as well. I began to spend time doing the tasks that required the most concentration (like writing) during the day when no one was at home. This is still the case. So, we all make adjustments.

The most important choice in any relationship is to choose to communicate, and to choose to learn the skill of communicating well. If I had communicated my plans better early on, there would have been less stress in the household. And if I had encouraged more discussion among the family, there would probably have been less stress in the household. I'm not sure — after all, teenagers are teenagers, and generally they don't want to communicate with mom and dad at all!

We're still working on some of these things. During the summers the kids still don't understand that I am not their chauffeur all day every day just because I am at home. Nor do they understand why they can't be in the office when I am working. My husband, on the other hand, does finally understand what it is I am working on, and the potential it has for our family (not to mention the potential for his early retirement!).

Setting others' expectations is not always easy. It is difficult to avoid making assumptions about others' current expectations. Start by asking what expectations others have, if you want an accurate picture. This could be as simple as "Do you understand what it is I'm interested in changing in my life? Have I explained it clearly?"

Once you know what their expectations are, then you can communicate with them about whether those current expectations are accurate or not. If they are not accurate, you can work on correcting the inaccuracies based on your knowledge of what will be happening, or what needs to take place.

> **Ask others, "What are your expectations?"**

Confirm, again by asking, what the other person's expectations include. Ask whether or not the other person understands what you have communicated, and what is expected of, and by, both of you. Remember, relationship expectations will further the relationship or destroy it, regardless of whether it is a personal or professional relationship.

It can be difficult to change habits we've had for a long time. If you are one of those people who has developed a habit of putting yourself down, or not giving yourself sufficient credit for your accomplishments, or not believing in yourself and your ability to succeed, this habit needs to be changed. The way to change is by beginning new habits of thinking and behaving, as outlined here. It takes consistent practice for a new behavior to become a habit. To create this new habit, use constant reminders of the power you have to succeed at the changes you have chosen.

We need to constantly be reminding ourselves of the positive traits and characteristics we have. It's often a struggle to believe in ourselves day in and day out. Even those who seem arrogant are usually just insecure, and the arrogance we see is a form of overcompensation on their part. There's a big difference between arrogance and confidence. The idea here is to be authentic, and truly understand what is valuable from our soul, or our innermost depths, in order to believe in ourselves and have the world see the value that we add by being here and doing what we do.

The more you create new habits of success that come from your heart—from your desire for a better life through making changes that count—the more others will view you as a successful person worthy of their time, effort, and help. Not all of the changes are easy, even when we want them very much, so they require consistency and perseverance in the approach.

As I've said before, these are relatively simple concepts, but easier in the elocution than the execution. Making positive self-expectation a habit and behaving as though success is inevitable are keys to ensuring that success. It will also ensure that others see success in us.

"Things alter for the worse spontaneously, if they be not altered for the better designedly."
Francis Bacon (1561-1626)

Chapter 11   Big Changes, Small Changes

The question of whether this method works for all changes has come up. I've found that it really makes no difference whether the path you are taking is life altering, or whether you are thinking about something of less magnitude, like redecorating a room.

The process is the same. It is similar to the Stephen Covey principle of "Begin with the end in mind," which is one of *The Seven Habits of Highly Effective People*. It is also the way one approaches project management—thinking about what it is that you are attempting to achieve, and then working "backward" on how you will get to that milestone of achievement.

Let's take the room redecoration idea for a minute. Perhaps the change you have decided upon is a change in your home. Your change choice is to make your kitchen and family living area less cluttered and more comfortable and inviting in order to induce more "togetherness" time for your family.

Where do you begin? You would begin with what style you would like to see in the room that would make everyone comfortable. You begin by envisioning what the room will be like when it is completed.

Assuming that you don't live alone (since one of the goals is more togetherness for your family) one of the next things you might do is discuss this idea and vision with your spouse and perhaps the rest of the family. This is expectation setting.

Once that vision is set and agreed to, if that is the way your family works together, the next step is to break down the components of what will be needed in order to create that look and feel for the room.

What furniture will be needed? What colors have you decided upon? Will the walls be painted or wallpapered? What type of flooring will be in the room? Will you need to change the window treatments? These are your choices.

The next step would be to research prices and availability for the items contained in your vision, determining whether the budget is sufficient to create your vision. If not, then it would be necessary to go back a step and rethink your vision. Again, discussion with your spouse and additional expectation setting would probably be in order.

If the budget works, then you would need to know lead times and installation timeframes, decide what you will do yourself and what you will pay a professional to do, and so on. These are examples of your opportunities to have the room you've chosen, as well as expectations of when it could be completed.

Cozier, more comfortable living space. More intimate family time. Having conversations rather than existing on the same couch in front of the television. Better family relationships. A place to encourage friendships. These are examples of what you would be facilitating.

Other types of giving from this choice could be providing the old furnishings to a shelter or other agency which helps underprivileged or indigent families.

As you can see in this example, all of the CORE elements are present. Frequently, you will find that the elements are each present more than once. That is, there will be more than one choice, many opportunities, multiple ways to be responsible, and setting and resetting of expectations, not always in that order.

Change =

Choice, Opportunity, Responsibility, Expectation

The elements, however, remain the same — regardless of the type of choice, or the impact of the changes you want to make.

"Only I can change my life. No one can do it for me."

Carol Burnett (1936-)

Chapter 12   Moving Forward—Action Causes Transformation!

In my experience, I have met many people with wonderful ideas for improving their lives and having abundance. I have also met many people who actually *have* abundance in their lives. What is the difference?

The difference is that the people who have abundance in their lives have taken those wonderful ideas they had, or that someone presented to them, and have acted upon them in order to achieve abundance.

The only way to move from having dreams and wonderful ideas to actually having abundance, is to take action. I like the acronym A-C-T.

Action Causes Transformation!

Remember, in order to move from having ideas and choices to actually creating the life you want, and creating transformation, action must be taken.

Once you get past the obstacles, or at least identify the fears and agree to set them aside and keep moving forward, you have to take the step to act on your choices. Usually this is the opportunity seeking phase of the Approach.

1. Make Choices
2. Identify Fears
3. Deal with Fears
4. Take Action!

In order to act on your ideas, there are more steps to be taken. These are the steps of Planning, Implementation, Test or Evaluation, Completion, and Review. They are all actions, and fall into the categories of Choice, Opportunity, Responsibility, and Expectation as well.

To make the connection, consider the chart on the following page. If you plan the stages of the change you want to make, not only will the potential for success be increased, but your choice will also make more sense to others. This will allow you to set proper expectations sooner and have more resources available as you move forward.

ACTION	STAGE	CORE ELEMENT
Envision end result	Planning	Choice
Research cost, time, energy	Planning	Choice
Decisions about methods, resources, budget, milestones, and deadlines	Planning	Choice, Opportunity
Find or receive affirmations	Planning	Opportunity
Identify the success criteria	Planning	Choice, Expectation
Talk with "stakeholders" — those who will be affected	Planning	Expectation
Identify who benefits from the outcome	Planning	Responsibility
Seek other beneficiaries	Implementation	Responsibility
Review goals regularly during implementation process; make changes as necessary to stay on target	Implementation, Test/Evaluation	Responsibility, Expectation
Review success criteria to determine completeness	Completion	Expectation
Make necessary adjustments	Implementation, Completion, Review	Choice, Opportunity
Complete change choice and success criteria — goal achieved	Completion, Review	Expectation
Celebrate!	Completion	The CORE Approach™

Are you beginning to see how actions have a significant impact on the ideas you have? Through the ages, there have been people society generally considers to be great thinkers. Some of these people have also been wonderful inventors, scientists, writers, and artists. They are the people who acted on their thoughts and ideas.

The world also needs philosophers and "think tank" members. Frequently, these are the people who create the idea, and there are others to whom the idea gets handed off to make it happen. Perhaps you are one of those people. Even in that case, there is still action to be taken. The thought or idea needs to be shared, and the right resources need to be brought into the discussion in order to make something happen with it.

So, regardless of whether you are a thinker or a doer, a creator or an implementer, there is action to be taken in order to achieve something with your ideas.

There's a wonderful book on the market called *Damn! Why Didn't I Write That?* by Marc McCutcheon. Marc writes about all the ideas that people have generated, and then acted upon, in order to make a lot of money or bring wonderful ideas to people.

Many of these concepts are funny, some are just downright silly (such as *The Duct Tape Book*), and many of them are good living ideas and knowledge, but all of them have created abundance of some sort because someone acted on an idea.

Have you ever had the following experience? You see a new product introduced on the market, or as in the example above, a new book come out, and think, "I was thinking about that same idea. I should have figured out how to turn it into a product (or book)." Most of us have had that experience. It happens a lot.

> **Failure to act will result
> in a lack of abundance in your life.**

It is that simple. Remember, abundance does not always mean money. You can have an abundance of anything that means something to you. Abundance, if you recall, means having more than enough. So, whether the abundance you are seeking (and we are all seeking some sort of abundance) is money, love, time, balance in our lives, caring, hugs, or friends, action has to be taken.

The only thing that will move you closer to attainment of the goals you have created as a result of your choices is taking action. You can have the most wonderful ideas and dreams, but if you never act on them, they will always remain ideas and dreams, and never become reality.

The types of action you take will depend on your choices. Big choices will potentially require bigger actions, and more of them. Smaller ideas and easier choices will require perhaps only one or two actions in order to make them a reality.

If you are finding that you are having difficulty taking action, determine the cause of the inertia. Chances are it is caused by an unresolved fear—in which case go back and read the early chapters of this book again—or a lack of knowledge of where to begin. If the inability to take action is caused by a lack of knowledge, identify resources to help you get started.

There are many consultants who can help, as well as websites you can use as resources, in addition to the myriad of self-help and home study courses provided by authors and speakers just like me. Spend an hour on the Internet or in your library, or have a conversation with a friend or significant other about where you are feeling stagnated, and you'll be surprised how much information you can gain in a very short time.

The main thing is to do something—A-C-T.

"It's not that some people have willpower and some don't. It's that some people are ready to change and others are not."

James Gordon, M.D.
Psychiatrist, professor,
founder of the Mind-Body Institute

Chapter 13   Getting Started and Keeping It Moving

I don't mind telling you that one of the most effective resources I have ever come across for undertaking any type of a project is, Steven Covey's *The Seven Habits of Highly Effective People*. I know I mentioned this once or twice before.

The Seven Habits of Highly Effective People is widely available in any number of bookstores and online sites for a nominal cost. It is well worth your time to read it and integrate the concepts into your thinking. The information you will need to order a copy is contained in the Resource section at the back of this book.

Mr. Covey wisely advises us to "Be Proactive." This is the first habit. And I've certainly reiterated that time and again, especially as related to the Opportunity element of The CORE Approach™.

That is all well and good, and it sounds great, but what about actually getting started? Where do I begin? Well, even before I ever read Mr. Covey's book, I was managing projects. In order to begin a project you have to understand what the expected end result will be. I was using this method before I ever heard the coined phrase "Begin with the End in Mind," which is the second of the seven habits.

So, in terms of getting started, you need to know where you are going. That's where those goals, and all the time you spent on choices, comes in. What does success look like to you? How will you know when you have achieved your goals?

Remember the redecorating example I used earlier? That example uses the same concepts but in a different type of project. What is your vision of the end result? If you are stuck in a "But this won't have an end—it will just keep growing" mode, then pick a date in time and put a vision on that date.

In other words, if I believe that my business, for instance, will just continue to grow, and there is no "end result" or limit to the success I can have, then I would perhaps take a 15-year view of the business. So my vision would be what the business goals achieved in 15 years would yield in dollars, value, lives affected, benefit for employees, and so on.

Once you've figured out how to get started, it is usually pretty easy to keep going for a while. Don't think for one minute, though, that those fears, obstacles, and even the paralysis won't ever come back. There will be times when it will come back and haunt you with a vengeance. These are the times that you need to get back to basics. Review the tools you've learned to use as a result of reading this book and other learning you have done to get to your goals.

For me, the times when fears return are the times that trigger me to pray more. I ask for more guidance from the spiritual realm as well as the practical, here-on-earth resources. I go back and re-evaluate the choices I have made and the opportunities I am pursuing and seeking to move further toward my goals.

I take stock at these times whether my giving program is sufficient, and whether I have set expectations for myself or others that are realistic.

These actions are the effort I make to ensure that I continue to be on the right path. Asking for guidance; reviewing intentions, choices, and goals; and making sure that affirmations continue to appear are all ways to confirm that the path being followed is the right path—it ensures that I haven't strayed or veered off course.

Any number of things can start the fears flooding back into your life and your choices. It is very easy to begin second guessing yourself, especially before you have total confidence and several successes to help you look back and say, "I can do this." It is common to be sidetracked, confused, and unfocused at times, especially when you find yourself in unfamiliar territory and realize that you might need more knowledge or resources than you currently have—even though you have already started down the path, and it could be even worse to turn back. Confusion can lead right back to the paralysis of fear if you let it.

"Toto, I don't think we're in Kansas anymore."

**Spoken by Dorothy to her dog,
upon landing in Munchkinland,
in the movie *The Wizard of Oz***

When confusion and fears show themselves, if you have done your homework, you will be prepared. Think ahead about what you will do if the fears come back. Arm yourself. Be prepared to take action. Remember that Action Causes Transformation. The action might be to wait, or to seek counsel, or to re-evaluate your choices and expectations, but these are, indeed, actions—especially when they have been consciously chosen as actions you will take to get past the fear, obstacle, or paralysis you are experiencing.

If you recall, I told you earlier in the book that I had trouble getting started with the writing, which was true enough. But getting started has never been my biggest problem with writing. Keeping the momentum has really been the greatest struggle.

The fears set back in or your focus changes, and the momentum comes to an abrupt halt. That is what was happening with me while I was writing this book. I wasn't having difficulty with fears—I'm pretty good at this point of just understanding them and pushing them away most of the time.

My setbacks had to do with how much I had going on, and how many "balls I was juggling in the air" at one time. When you try to do too many things at one time, the focus gets lost, and the momentum cannot continue.

For me, trying to write in what I consider to be dribs and drabs of time—an hour here or there—really is not productive. I do better with four to ten hours of quiet, uninterrupted time. Now, when you consider that I have a husband, four children between the ages of 14 and 23 years, two cats, and a backyard garden that just calls to me in the spring and summer, getting those blocks of time is next to impossible.

A resetting of expectations was definitely in order. I had to adjust—not an easy thing for me on this task. I can adjust to a lot, for a lot of causes, but this one was definitely tough. Only getting down to a printing deadline forced me to bend my habits and preferences and work through some difficult weeks at my home office to get the final writing and editing completed.

But, here it is—you hold in your hand my book—proof that with focus and perseverance, taking action and keeping the momentum going is possible.

Getting started—once you have a plan and a system, or set of concepts like The CORE Approach™ to follow—is the easy part. One step at a time, you review the concepts and do the exercises to begin the process of creating the life you want.

Think about making conscious choices, based on your passions. Find or create your opportunities, identifying what knowledge you might need to keep moving forward.

Have the courage to set a strategy for creating abundance and be responsible about giving as you further your progress toward your goals. Set and continue to reset expectations all along the way, maintaining the focus on the goals you have set as a result of your choices.

Persevere through the difficult times and setbacks and temporary lapses back into the fear state. With time, using these concepts begins to become second nature, and you will find yourself teaching others about them as well. This will be part of giving responsibly as you become proficient at The CORE Approach™.

My prayer and fervent wish is that you have gained from this book knowledge and a useful approach for changing your life and creating the life you want.

"Human beings, who are almost unique in having the ability to learn from the experience of others, are also remarkable for their apparent disinclination to do so."

Douglas Adams (1952-2001)
in *Last Chance to See*

Chapter 14   Case Studies

A book like *Change Your Life! The CORE Approach™ to Creating the Life You Want* would not be complete without case studies. I have tried to provide the reader with exercises and precise explanations of the concepts. I also wanted to utilize as many of the learning capabilities of the reader audience as possible in order to have the most robust learning experience.

Now that you've read through the book, you've understood the concepts, and have begun to think about your own use of the elements of The CORE Approach™, you have the background for understanding how it can be used in your own life scenarios.

By viewing case studies, you can understand real-life examples of the application of the concepts. When deeper understanding exists, the chance of the continued use of the concepts is greater, thereby providing a higher probability of making each of the CORE elements a habit.

Integrating positive habits into our personalities will prove extremely valuable when our goals are success oriented. And whose goals are not success oriented? Do you know anyone who sets goals, intending to fail? If such people exist, I have not met any of them.

If the intention of setting our goals is success, we use the CORE elements and their related actions, and we can see these elements in the workings of real people's lives, we have created a success plan. Using examples from others, each of you can then begin to make connections to situations in your lives, and understand how The CORE Approach™ is applicable.

Case Study #1:   The Restaurant

I had the privilege of working with a client who was a successful restaurant owner. Let's call him Ralph. Ralph had a very profitable small restaurant that served breakfast, lunch, and dinner. Ralph could be seen cooking, taking orders, chatting with customers, or running the cash register on any given day. His wife was the hostess and as his children grew, they could also be found on the premises, washing dishes, preparing food, or waiting tables. Ralph's Restaurant (not the real name of the restaurant) closed early, had no bar or liquor license, and was considered by its customers to be a family restaurant—very child friendly.

Ralph's Restaurant frequently had a waiting list, with customers lined up through the parking lot waiting for a table. His success was obvious. Ralph's Restaurant had been in business for 15 years, and was a known establishment in the area. Everyone knew what you were talking about if you mentioned Ralph's Restaurant.

Ralph became my client when, through discussions, he realized that I had a strategy that could help him with a problem he had. His problem was that he wanted a chain of Ralph's Restaurants, but he only knew how to run a restaurant. He didn't know how to build a chain or run a corporation.

For me, Ralph was a blessing. What I mean is this: he knew how much he didn't know. Many people who decide to follow their dream have no idea how much they don't know about what it will take to achieve.

So we set to work. I explained to Ralph that just the act of making this choice, and working on the plan would be a major adjustment to his lifestyle. He would have to identify all the choices that accompany the choice to expand, the opportunities he would have, how he and his business would continue to be responsible, and the expectation setting he would have to do around the changes. When he understood the magnitude of all of this, and continued to want to move forward, we did just that.

First things being first, he talked with his family, and then we talked with his family. Things would change. Ralph would be busy with business planning, so a cook would have to be hired and trained. Other staff, including family members, would have to learn to make decisions because Ralph would not always be right there to help them or make the decision himself. Their family life would change because of the shift in responsibilities and the hours Ralph would be spending on his planning, and eventually implementation.

In the interest of not boring you to death if you are not a restaurant owner, and in keeping the book to a number of pages that is not intimidating, I have summarized these choices. This is by no means a complete listing of all that we did. If your life goal is to own a chain of restaurants, please do not consider this a how-to manual. This is a case study, and as such, is a summary of the thought process, tasks, events, and outcome.

The choices alone took a lot of time. We made a list that included pages and pages of potential choices. Some of the choices were:

- How many restaurants would be in this chain?
- Would all of the locations be similar demographic areas?
- Would they all look alike?
- Would they buy or lease the properties, or some combination?
- Would they eventually franchise, or hold the ownership of all of the individual restaurants?
- Did he have sufficient funds to move forward or would he have to borrow to make his dreams come true?
- How quickly would this growth take place? How many restaurants would be launched in what period of time?

- Would purchasing for décor and corporate items be centralized?
- How would food purchasing be handled? (This is difficult to centralize if the restaurants are not in the same geographic areas.)
- Would the menus be consistent across the chain?
- How would staff recruitment, training, manuals, etc. be handled?

We talked about the other choices that had to do with building the corporation, not just the restaurants. These choices included brainstorming answers to questions about whether Ralph had the business experience to run a corporation, or whether he would have to hire help; what type of culture he wanted to create with the chain; how much he knew about marketing, branding, and creating the strategy for these things; how he wanted to handle corporate-wide programs of giving; corporation-wide systems for computers, communication, and more.

Once we had come to decisions about the seemingly unending choices Ralph needed to make, and had set goals for the company, it was time to explore opportunities. Again, lists of choices for opportunities were made.

Whether to hire a marketing and advertising firm to develop a campaign, and how to select real estate markets in which to seek properties for new restaurants were just two of the opportunities to expand that were explored.

In the midst of all of this, the idea of expanding the existing restaurant was also explored, as was the idea of packaging some of the food being made in the restaurant, and having a shop nearby that would sell a Ralph's Restaurant line of packaged foods. There were more choices to make and discussions to have in regard to how many things should get Ralph's focus at one time. Remember, in order to succeed, there needs to be continuous focus on the goal to be achieved. Digression and dilution are contraindicated when working toward an aggressive goal. The result was that we maintained a more narrow focus on the restaurants alone.

Throughout this process, Ralph was constantly having to set his own expectations for how much he could take on (or, at times, re-setting those expectations). He also had to work with his spouse, family, and staff to ensure that they understood what he was try-ing to do, and how each choice would affect them. Communication and expectation setting is an ongoing process.

There were a number of "obstacle" discussions. I spent long hours with Ralph talking about his beliefs and doubts about whether he could achieve his dream of having a chain of Ralph's Restaurants. I spent one-on-one time with his wife to help her understand when he was unable to do so. Sometimes it is easier for an outside party to explain something because that person isn't so close, and doesn't get side-tracked by the history and the baggage that exists in the relationship.

I spent time with family members and staff members, helping them understand what it might mean to them in the short term — picking up some of the slack left by Ralph doing other things. I spent even more time with them, though, discussing what oppor-tunities for their own growth would come from the choices Ralph was making. Ralph's dream was opening up a whole new world of possibilities for people who never thought some of those opportunities would come their way.

I taught the interested family and staff members The CORE Ap-proach™ as well, and they began to use it to help them make conscious choices about their ideas and dreams, too.

Ralph's Restaurant was already a Food Drive participating facil-ity. There were more choices about responsibility for Ralph, too. Was the Food Drive to be his only "giving" program? There were discussions about many of his options and choices in regard to responsibility, including:

- Would the Red Cross Food Drive be a consistent giving program across the corporation, with all restaurants in the chain participating?
- Other opportunities for giving food were discussed — local food kitchens and homeless shelters, Meals on Wheels programs, and so forth.
- Other giving choices — nonfood-related — were also discussed: Would they hire developmentally disabled individuals, or veterans? Would they sponsor Little League or other community sports programs? Would they sponsor fund drives from national organizations which would allow them to involve customers and staff in fundraising and participating in community events, like the local walks, runs, and bicycle races promoted by some of these organizations?

The result of all of these discussions, choice decisions, responsibility decisions, and expectation conversations was that in six months' time, we had a complete business plan and marketing plan for making Ralph's dreams come to fruition. In addition, Ralph's family was not only still a happy family, but also excited about the prospects of growth.

In less than a year, Ralph had opened a second Ralph's Restaurant, had contracts in hand for two more, and was discussing a franchising opportunity with his former cook, who was by then the manager of one of the existing restaurants.

Case Study #2:   L. Frank Baum, Author

He didn't have a vision that included financial independence through box office sales, royalties, and retail lines for years to come. He didn't envision himself becoming a multi-millionaire and having one of his products become a staple of the American population. He just wanted to write stories for children.

Perhaps you never knew the name of the man, but there is a good chance that you have known the name of one of his stories for a very long time, even though you might not know the real name of the story.

The story is *The Wizard of Oz*. That incredible movie has been shown year after year since 1939, when MGM brought the story of Dorothy, the lost girl from Kansas, to the big screen.

The original name of the story is *The Wonderful Wizard of Oz*, and although the story bears significant resemblance to the movie, reading the story is a very different experience from watching the movie.

The man behind the story, if not behind the curtain, was L. Frank Baum. Born in 1856, in a town near Syracuse, New York, Lyman Frank Baum knew by the time he was five years old that he did not like his first name, and was from then on called by his middle name, Frank.

Since Frank was born with some health difficulties, including a heart ailment, he was held back from strenuous childhood play, and therefore probably spent more time with his imagination than might have been typical for other children. He loved fairy stories and reading. He did not, however, like the witches and goblins that frightened him in the stories, so he determined to write a fairy tale that was different.

Frank Baum wrote as a journalist and playwright and worked for a time as an actor. His father owned opera houses situated from New York to Pennsylvania, which enabled him to follow these choices for his livelihood. It was clear that he had a passion for storytelling and that he was making choices about his outlets for this passion in his writing and acting and producing.

He married his wife in 1882, and when they started their family, Frank decided to settle down in Syracuse. He worked in the family businesses and experienced some setbacks. They sold the business and moved west.

In Aberdeen, Frank opened Baum's Bazaar, a general store. There he had a frequent audience of youngsters who came in for penny candy or ice cream, and he told his stories in the afternoons. The economy suffered, and they lost the store. Frank then went into journalism again, selling advertising for the magazine and newspaper. It is said that he would sit on the side of the street with the children telling stories when they stopped him while making his rounds to advertisers.

In 1893, they went to Chicago where Frank looked for work. He worked as a reporter for the *Evening Post* and then as a traveling salesman for a china company. He continued to tell stories of far-off lands with compelling characters to his children and their friends. It was his mother-in-law who eventually mentioned that he should write these stories down.

While traveling, he began to do just that. Before long, he had numerous stories captured on paper. He used his journalism contacts to identify someone who would publish his writing, and in 1897 *Mother Goose in Prose*, by Frank Baum, was published.

When his health failed and he could no longer travel extensively, he started another magazine called *The Show Window*. He met William Denslow at the Press Club, and the two co-authored *Father Goose, His Story.*

After other collaborations, and through continuing his story-telling with the children, the story of *The Emerald City* was born. By now Frank had learned to write his stories down. When he took the story to The Hill Company, they loved the story but not the title. Eventually, it became *The Wonderful Wizard of Oz.*

Frank wanted to write a different type of fairy tale. He borrowed the sorcerer and sorceress and magic-type characters from some European stories; the scarecrow was actually a character from his dreams — one who chased him in his dreams as a child. It is inter-esting that he turned this negative image from his childhood into a positive image of friend for Dorothy in his story.

The Baum and Denslow partnership broke up over the moviemaking of *The Wizard of Oz*, and each went on with his own career and interests. Frank produced seventeen sequels to *The Wonderful Wizard of Oz.*

In 1908 he produced a traveling film show called "Fairylogue and Radio Plays" which was a failure. Semi-retired, but still writing — and in debt — he turned to his garden for solace, and became an award-winning amateur horticulturist.

It is told that in later years, as his health continued to fail, he con-tinued to write, even through the pain he obviously felt. One quote I found in a biographical summary, attributed to the 1961 *To Please a Child, Biography of L. Frank Baum, Royal Historian of Oz,* was, "Although few traces of agony are detectable in his work, there were many times when the tears would stream from his eyes and wet the paper as he wrote."

He continued to write under his own name and using pseudonyms, and enjoyed a level of prosperity from this. He died in 1919; his last Oz sequel, *Glinda of Oz*, was published posthumously.

Now that I have given you a synopsis of the life of L. Frank Baum, you might be wondering about the point. Why did I use L. Frank Baum as a case study for The CORE Approach™?

Think about his story. He made *choices*, some based on his health, and some based on his passion, but they were conscious choices. He loved storytelling throughout his life, no matter what else he was doing. His *passion* continued to shine through all else that he did—journalism, managing theatres and magazines, acting, selling—he told stories and wrote wherever he went. He sought *opportunities* in every relationship.

Although never in excellent health, he *gave* his time to children whenever they asked, or whenever he could, to make their days brighter with his stories. He chose to preserve those stories by giving them, in writing and in film, to the rest of the world. His sense of *responsibility*, even though he may not have called it that, came through always. At times it appears he continued to give even though his infirmities caused him great pain.

He always took care of his family by working at various jobs and companies wherever they lived, in Syracuse, Aberdeen, Chicago, and then later in parts of California. His family always knew that he would take care of them, and they always knew that no matter how tired he was, or how ill, he would always tell his stories. He set his own *expectations* for what he wanted to achieve and he set their *expectations* by his actions. The legacy he left tells the story of the expectations he set while he walked on this earth.

This man's passion for stories and his talent for portraying them would fuel his enthusiasm to achieve the goals set by his life choices. Although Frank Baum never heard of The CORE Approach™, he lived it by his example.

Appendix: An Overview of The CORE Approach™

The CORE Approach ™ is a step-by-step guide to the principles that can help you Change Your Life!

Think about the following key concepts:

> **What is holding you back?**

> **What will enable you to move over, through, or around the obstacles?**

> **Give up the fear.**

Do I have the knowledge I need?

What is my passion?

How strong is my courage?

Why am I not happy with my life?

Why can't I just be content with
the way things are?

CHOICE

Choice #1: *Choose to make choices.*
Make good ones.

Choice #2: *Choose your values.*

Choice #3: *Choose your goals.*

Choice #4: *Choose to be aware.*

Choice #5: *Choose your priorities.*

Choice #6: *Choose to be patient.*

Choice #7: *Choose to persevere.*

Choice #8: *Choose to be intentional.*

You can accomplish the goals you set for yourself.

OPPORTUNITY

Opportunities are always around you.

It is your responsibility to find or create
opportunities for the life you want.

Where will I find an opportunity today?

Opportunities may not arrive in the way,
shape, or form that you expect.

RESPONSIBILITY

Giving is our right and our responsibility.

We receive exponentially more than we give.

How can I help?

Where can I help?

EXPECTATIONS

What are your expectations?

What are your expectations of yourself?

Change the way you expect
yourself to react.

Your reactions are your choice
and your responsibility.

Change your behavior by
changing your expectations.

Set the expectation for the behavior you
want to see in others.

Ask others, "What are your expectations?"

ACTION

Change =

Choice, Opportunity, Responsibility,
Expectation

Action Causes Transformation!

Failure to act will result in a
lack of abundance in your life.

NOTES

Resource Guide and Recommended Reading

Embracing FEAR and Finding the Courage to Live Your Life
Thom Rutledge

The Why Are You Here Café
John Strelecky

The Seven Habits of Highly Effective People
Stephen R. Covey

The Power of Focus
Mark Victor Hansen

The Aladdin Factor
Mark Victor Hansen and Jack Canfield

Who Do You Think You Are? The Berkeley Personality Profile
Keith Harary, Ph.D. and Eileen Donahue, Ph.D

The Art of Abundance
Candy Paul

Please Understand Me II
David Keirsey

Conversations on Success
Insight Publishing

The Power of Focus for Women
Fran Hewitt and Les Hewitt

Titles by the Author

Book - *Change Your Life! The CORE Approach™ to Creating the Life You Want*

$17.95

Audio CDs – The CORE Approach™ to Success
(4 CD set) $89.95

Audio CDs – The CORE Approach™ to Entrepreneuring
$149.95

Audio CDs – The CORE Approach™ to Money Management
$119.95

Audio CDs – The CORE Approach™ to Career Choices and Changes $149.95

Also Featured In:

Conversations on Success, Insight Publishing $19.95

Quick Order Form

FAX orders: 215-616-0673
E-MAIL orders: info@verisassociates.com
POSTAL orders:
Veris Publishing, 600 Collins Ave., Lansdale, PA 19446
TELEPHONE: 610-283-0948

Please send the following books or Audio CD sets:
(I understand that I may return any of them for a full refund
if I am not completely satisfied.)

_____

_____

_____

Please send me free additional information on:
☐ Other books ☐ Seminars ☐ Other Audio CD sets

Name:_____

Address:_____

City:_____State:_____Zip:_____

Telephone:_____e-mail:_____

Shipping: $4.00 for first book or CD set; $2.00 for each
 additional product shipped to the same address

Payment: ☐ Visa   ☐ MasterCard

Card Number:_____

Name on Card:_____Exp. Date:____

Address on card (if different from above):

_____

City:_____State:_____Zip:_____